21 Secrets of the Universe

Rikka Zimmerman

Seeds of
Consciousness
Press

©2011 Rikka Zimmerman.
All rights reserved.
ISBN: 978-1-4507-6657-9
Published by Seeds of Consciousness Press
Cover Design by Christine Gressianu
Cover Illustration by K'lei Legerski
Interior Design by Liz Mrofka

Table of Contents

Acknowledgments 8

Forward 9

Day 1 10
How to use the Access Consciousness™ "Clearing Statement"

Day 2 24
Living in and as the question

Day 3 31
What if you are far more psychic and aware then
you've ever given yourself credit for?

Day 4 36
Having ease with your awareness

Day 5 40
Having ease with your body's awareness

Day 6 43
Getting out of judgment

Day 7 51
What if you lost your capacity to judge?

Day 8 55
Your body is your greatest conscious facilitator

Day 9 59
Getting out of the wrongness of you — you are an alien

Day 10 72
Choosing your life in 10 second increments

Day 11 76
Choosing your life in 10 second increments and following the energy

Day 12.. 83
Choosing in 10 second increments; what energies you choose for your life

Day 13.. 88
Validation of other peoples' realities

Day 14.. 96
The secret ingredient for your life is YOU!

Day 15.. 105
What if you are a Superhero and don't know it?

Day 16.. 112
Choosing your life in 10 second increments, being
in total allowance and letting go of control

Day 17.. 118
Contributing to you

Day 18.. 123
Creating a nurturing, caring, kind, expansive and joyful
relationship with your body

Day 19.. 133
Choosing for your body in 10 second increments

Day 20.. 138
Having the relationship you truly desire

Day 21.. 152
The Love of your life is YOU!

Quick Start Guide to Consciousness...................... 161

Glossary... 173

Access Consciousness™ books............................. 175

Access Consciousness™ seminars, workshops and classes.......... 176

More information.. 177

There is only one person powerful enough to stop you . . . .

There is only one person powerful enough to set you free . . . .

And give YOU everything you desire out of YOUR life.

Are you willing to choose it?

Acknowledgments

I give a special thank you to Gary Douglas, founder of Access Consciousness™, and Dr. Dain Heer. Every tool, process and piece of information in this book has come directly from Access Consciousness™ and my experience with it. Thank you for seeing me when I didn't know how. Thank you for being willing to be what we were all not willing to be, so that you could show us how to be it. You have given me a gift beyond words... without you, I wouldn't have me. If you like the life you receive from this book you're going to love the Access Consciousness™ core classes, and everything else Access Consciousness™ has to offer @ www.accessconsciousness.com.

Forward

Consider this book your new best friend . . . .

Your companion for the next 21 days . . . .

Your comrade . . . your confidant . . . .

You will whisper on the pages your secret dreams . . . .

And it will show you how to make those dreams come true . . . .

At times it will be the love of your life,

And at times you may feel frustrated as it challenges your reality

and want to throw it away . . . .

Just keep going . . . .

And after this journey . . . .

You will be a new YOU!

What if this was the beginning of you actually having the life that you truly desire?

Day I

How to use the Access Consciousness™ "Clearing Statement"

DAILY EXERCISE: Using "The Clearing Statement" to undo any points of view that aren't working for you."

STEP 1: Take a deep breath and ask . . . .
If I could actually get anything and everything I desire out of my life, and nothing was impossible, what would I ask for?

❑ _____

❑ _____

❑ _____

❑ _____

❑ _____

❑ _____

❑ _____

❑ _____

Now we can begin. Your request has been made. Ask and you shall receive.

Access Consciousness™ & How it Works

Access Consciousness™ is a set of tools and processes that can change anything that is not working for you in your life. It was founded by Gary Douglas and has been changing peoples' lives all over the world for over 20 years. It works . . . because you work. It is based on the question. As an Access Consciousness™ facilitator I ask you questions to empower you to know what you know, because there is not another being on the planet that knows what you know. If I were to give you "my" answer for your life I would be robbing you from the gift you truly are. There is not another being that receives what you receive nor has your particular awareness and gift for the world. You are unique unto yourself.

Never believe anything that I or anyone else tells you. Always ask it in a question for yourself to find out what is true for you. Access Consciousness™ can't do anything to you, or for you, but it can give you an opportunity to change you. Also, it is designed to bypass your logical mind. So if you don't understand, it's okay. If your logical mind had all the answers to your life, wouldn't you have everything figured out already? If something doesn't make sense to you, read it over and over and then run the clearing statement and it will become clear to you.

If you would like to get the most out of this information, take your time. Grab a hot cup of tea or coffee. Sit in your favorite chair. Digest each secret. Take deep breaths. Look out the window. Contemplate how this information might apply to your life. Ponder all of the information you are going to be introduced to throughout this 21 day program. Also, all of this information is built step by step. Therefore, if you skip ahead you will be missing information and it could be confusing for you. Just in case you purchased the book by itself you may wish to also purchase the *21 Secrets of the Universe* Complete Package. There are 21 hours of audios, a 63-card deck and more goodies that will lead you through this book step by step. You can purchase these at www.21secretsoftheUniverse.com.

Before we get started let us get a few of the basics down. When I say, "Ask and you shall receive is one of the truths of the Universe" does that make you feel lighter or heavier? Lighter, huh? That is because the truth will always make you feel lighter and what is not true will always make you feel heavier. When somebody says something that's true, your whole body and being lighten and it feels like a big expansive deep breath, "Ahh". That's how you know what is true for you. And if something feels heavy or sticky that something is not true for you.

SECRET OF THE UNIVERSE:
The truth will always make you feel lighter and a lie will always make you feel heavier.

This is how we will navigate through your life to find out what is true for you. This book is not about choosing what "Access Consciousness™" wants you to choose. It's about choosing what works for you. "Access Consciousness™" doesn't desire you to choose anything. It is a set of tools for you to use to undo everywhere you have created limiting beliefs so you can choose whatever it is you truly desire.

What if you are the creator of everything in your life? Does that make you feel lighter? If you are the creator of your life, can you change any part of it? Yeah, huh? So what I'll do over these 21 days is ask you questions that bring up the energy of these limiting beliefs and then run what we call "The Clearing Statement." This essentially is asking you to go back in time to whenever you created the limitation and undo the seed you planted and everything you've created based on that seed ever since. It's like flushing the energetic toilet and undoing everything you've done to limit you, which then changes the past, present, and future.

Note: Can the truth be destroyed? The truth is, you are the oneness and consciousness of all things. Can that be destroyed? No. So no matter what you destroy and un-create all you are going to let go of is all of the judgments that are holding the limitations in place. Also, no matter what you let go of, you can always make the same choice you had made before the clearing. You could go through this whole program, let go of every limitation and still choose the same exact life if you desired.

The Access Consciousness™ Clearing Statement is as follows;
Right, Wrong, Good, Bad, POC, POD, All 9, Shorts, Boys and Beyonds™™.

It is short-speak for a series of questions that change the energy. That way we don't have to go through each of these questions whenever we would like to change something. This clearing statement can be used to change the energy of anything; it's a fill-in-the-blank system. Let's get started using this clearing statement and change the energy in regards to having no money.

"Right and Good" stands for:
How have you made having no money right, good, perfect, and/or correct?

So check it out. How have you made having no money right? Are there lifetimes where you've been a monk and denounced all your worldly possessions and then thought,

"Now I finally have me". So you think the only way to actually have you is to eliminate money from your life. How else have you made <u>having no money</u> right? Have you ever been out to dinner with a friend and he or she is complaining about the economy and how they are broke and their business is barely surviving? Now, if you said "Actually I have tons of money and my business is doing better than ever!" Does he or she like you, or not like you? Exactly. That's also where you've made <u>having no money</u> right. Also we are taught, "Money is the root of all evils." If you don't want to be evil you eliminate money from your life so you can be good. Those are just a few of the belief systems and limitations that you have bought from this reality that make <u>having no money</u> right. So everything that brings up for you will you destroy and un-create all that?
Right, Wrong, Good, Bad, POC, POD, All 9, Shorts, Boys and Beyonds™.

"Wrong and Bad" stands for:
How have you made <u>having no money</u> wrong, terrible, awful, mean and vicious?

Okay, well, that's pretty easy, just look at your bank account.

How much do you go to the wrongness of you based on the money you don't have? Everything that brings up, will you destroy and un-create it all? Right, Wrong, Good, Bad, POC, POD, All 9, Shorts, Boys and Beyonds™.

What we're doing is clearing all of the energy that doesn't allow you to have what you desire. I had a friend who wanted to charge $250 an hour for a session. She had tried to raise her rates in the past and every time anyone asked her, "How much do you charge?" She would think about saying "I'm $250 an hour," and her throat would close up and her whole Universe would contract. She would then fall back on her usual rates and say "I'm $90 an hour." She knew that for her phenomenal, expansive, fun-filled life she would be charging $250 an hour, except every time she went to go choose it all of the judgments and conclusions that she had created about charging $250 an hour would come up and stop her. That is the energy we are clearing with the clearing statement. After she started using "The Clearing Statement" she can now say, "Yes, I charge $250 an hour!" and nothing comes up in her Universe. How cool is that?

If you could charge any amount of money for your product or service, what would that be? Ask your product or service how much it would like to be. Everything that doesn't allow that will you destroy and un-create all that? Right, Wrong, Good, Bad, POC, POD, All 9, Shorts, Boys and Beyonds™.

All 9" stands for:

1. How does <u>having no money</u> diminish you?

You diminish your worth depending on how much money you don't have. Then you create more judgments depending on how old you are, how much debt you've created, or how much money you've lost. This can affect every area of your life. You might not allow yourself to receive a relationship because you don't have money. You think, "I'm only as valuable as how many thousands of dollars I have in the bank." Or if you have hundreds, then you feel really good about yourself, huh? Or, if you're in debt, then you feel really, really good about yourself . . . NOT!

Everything that brings up for you and everywhere you've used <u>having no money</u> to diminish you will you destroy and un-create all that?
Right, Wrong, Good, Bad, POC, POD, All 9, Shorts, Boys and Beyonds™.

2. How does <u>having no money</u> make you absolutely, totally, irrevocably, infinitely, utterly and eternally meaningless?

Have you met people that are overdrawn in their account and can't pay their rent? No matter what they try, to do they won't allow themselves to receive money. It feels like they are in a constant mobius strip, looping and looping on the biggest problem in their life. Does it also seem like no matter what, they never allow themselves to change their life and have money? What if that was more about the energy they are willing to be and receive than anything else? Since everything is energy, if we actually change the energy, literally, money would show up.

Everything that brings up for you and everywhere you've used <u>having no money</u> to make you absolutely, totally, irrevocably, infinitely, utterly and eternally meaningless will you destroy and un-create all that?
Right, Wrong, Good, Bad, POC, POD, All 9, Shorts, Boys and Beyonds™.

3. What are the rewards that make <u>having no money</u> right, good, perfect and/or correct?

One example of a good reward for <u>having no money</u> is being liked by other people. If you have no money, more people like you, because you are choosing the same limitation they are choosing and are validating their reality. If you're hanging around with someone who doesn't allow themselves to have money and you allow yourself to have money, sometimes they don't like you. If you make yourself impoverished like everybody else then you're just like them, and that makes them happy. Another reward would be fitting in and feeling like everyone else. What else would be some of the rewards for <u>having no money</u>? Some people actually create money as the biggest problem in their life. If money is a problem for you and, if you have no money, then you have eliminated the biggest problem of your life! If you don't have it, you can't lose it!

Also, if you have judgments of people who have money (such as they are selfish or self-centered), then once you eliminate money from your life you'll never have to be any of those judgments! Isn't that cool? NOT!

Everything that brings up for you and everywhere you have felt rewarded by the money you don't have will you destroy and un-create it all?
Right, Wrong, Good, Bad, POC, POD, All 9, Shorts, Boys and Beyonds™.

4. In regards to <u>having no money</u> what are the rewards that make this wrong, bad, terrible, awful, mean and vicious?

Do you have a joyful life? Do you wake up every morning excited to be, excited to receive, and excited to generate a phenomenal life that's beyond anything you can currently imagine? If you have a joyful life does this reality receive you? Or do people feel more comfortable when there is a level of wrongness and judgment in your Universe? And, if you go to lunch and laugh hysterically or joyfully, do people re-ceive and enjoy the laughter or do they tell you to be quiet? Do you get kicked out or do they ask you "What drug are you on, because you're too happy?" Isn't that amaz-ing? We create this wrong, terrible and awful energy in order to fit into this reality.

Everywhere you've had no money so that you could create the energy of your life as wrong, bad, terrible, awful, mean and vicious energy will you destroy and un-create all that?
Right, Wrong, Good, Bad, POC, POD, All 9, Shorts, Boys and Beyonds™.

5. As <u>having no money,</u> what choices have we made or are we making?

Wow, right? If you don't allow yourself to receive money there are choices you are making in order to create <u>having no money</u>. One example of a choice to <u>have no money</u> is lowering your prices on a sliding scale in order to accommodate other people's limitations around receiving money? Instead of actually creating a financial situation that works for you in your life and makes you feel excited to wake up in the morning, you will accommodate other people and end up resenting them as clients, not in your best interest. Another example of a choice you make to not have money is upholding the "one man or one woman Universe," which means you do everything yourself. Let's say you charge $250 an hour and it takes you four hours to clean your house. How much does it cost you to clean your house? $1,000. Instead of paying a maid $60 you'll charge yourself $1000 to clean your own house. Also, if you have ever said, "I would, if I had the money," you are making money greater than choice. What if it was a choice to have money? A lot of people use not having money as a way to eliminate their choices.

All of the choices you make that create you <u>having no money</u>, will you destroy and un-create all that?
Right, Wrong, Good, Bad, POC, POD, All 9, Shorts, Boys and Beyonds™.

6. As <u>having no money</u>, what creations create the commitments to the creation of our limitations?

You're actually committed to <u>having no money</u> or else you would have it. There are parts of your life where you love having a problem. You may be committed to feeling like everyone else. You may be committed to a relationship or a friendship and that relationship or friendship would change if you had tons of money.

Everywhere you are committed to the creation of the limitation of <u>having no money</u> will you destroy and un-create it all?
Right, Wrong, Good, Bad, POC, POD, All 9, Shorts, Boys and Beyonds™.

7. As <u>having no money</u>, how many limitations of dimensionality hold this in existence?

Everything that brings up, will you destroy and un-create it all?
Right, Wrong, Good, Bad, POC, POD, All 9, Shorts, Boys and Beyonds™.

8. As <u>having no money</u>, how much control, definition, limitation, form, structure, significance, linearities, and concentricities of you are you using to hold this in existence?

How much are you controlling your life to guarantee and ensure you never allow yourself to receive more money than you know what to do with? Isn't that weird? But do you feel like if you got more clients, more business, and more money—it would mean more work, less time for you, less time with your family and more to "deal" with? So you create this idea that if you had more money, more business and more clients you'd have to work harder. So if you don't wish to work harder you'll never allow money to show up because money = work.

Everything that brings up, will you destroy and un-create it all?
Right, Wrong, Good, Bad, POC, POD, All 9, Shorts, Boys and Beyonds™.

Have you defined yourself as someone who has more money than they can spend and never enough? Or have you defined yourself as somebody who is right for barely surviving? One of the biggest ways in which people limit the amount of money that can show up in their life is by making the amount of money they have "right." When they do that the Universe cannot give them more.

Have you ever made the amount of money that it takes for you to survive for the month in the first two weeks and in weeks three and four the money stopped showing up? That's because you told the Universe, okay I'm good, which means okay, I've concluded that this is enough for me now. I don't need to receive anything else, so stop sending clients and money my way, as if you have to "need" money in order to receive it.

Everything that brings up, and everywhere you've made the amount of money you have right, will you destroy and un-create it all?
Right, Wrong, Good, Bad, POC, POD, All 9, Shorts, Boys and Beyonds™.

How many limitations do you have that create you <u>having no money</u>? Limitations are a lot of different things. They are any kind of conclusion or judgment. Let me ask you this, "How much of the gift that you are do you allow yourself to receive?"

What percentage?_____. If you don't see the gift that you are and you are charging for your time from your point of view, you have no valuable product. There is no product or service. And there is no gift for their life because you never allow yourself to see it.

Everything that doesn't allow you to perceive, know, be and receive the gift you truly be will you destroy and un-create it all?
Right, Wrong, Good, Bad, POC, POD, All 9, Shorts, Boys and Beyonds™.

How many forms, structures and significances of you are you using to create the energy of "not having" money or "wanting" money as you and your life? "Want" actually has twenty-seven different definitions that mean to lack and one that means "to desire." Have you ever have made money significant by how much you want it? When you make something significant, you are actually creating a separation between you and you having it. If you had it, you would never create the significance of not having it. Would a billionaire say I "want" money? No, you never hear a billionaire say "want" because that's not part of their point of view around money. They actually allow themselves to have it. It's like breathing for them. It's like, "Of course there's tons of money being funneled into my account all the time."

Everywhere you have made money significant, will you destroy and un-create all that?
Right, Wrong, Good, Bad, POC, POD, All 9, Shorts, Boys and Beyonds™.

What if you allowed receiving money and having money to be like breathing? Do you deserve to breathe or do you just breathe? When you wake up every day knowing you have money and more money is coming, because it always does, it does. Your point of view actually creates your reality. How many points of view do you have that money is hard to get, hard to come by, or out there and you keep trying to get it and it never shows up? Every one of those points of view is creating exactly that.

All the points of view that you have that don't allow you to receive more money, will you destroy and un-create all of them?
Right, Wrong, Good, Bad, POC, POD, All 9, Shorts, Boys and Beyonds™.

9. As <u>having no money</u> what are you unwilling to destroy that holds this in existence?

Are you in a relationship or friendship where you share your limitations around not having money? Let me ask you this. If you were making billions of dollars would that change the relationship? For some people it would. This is one of the things that you're unwilling to destroy that holds this in existence. It might be you're unwilling to destroy problems in your life so you keep money as a problem to make sure that you feel like everybody else.

So everything you're unwilling to destroy that holds <u>having no money</u> in existence, will you destroy and un-create it all?
Right, Wrong, Good, Bad, POC, POD, All 9, Shorts, Boys and Beyonds™.

P.O.C. stands for the point of creation:
What we're looking at applying our consciousness to, is the point of creation, or the POC, of where we planted the seed of limitation. What you're doing is going back in time, to where you planted the seed and destroying the seed which then destroys everything you've built based on it ever since then. So that's the concept we're referring to when we talk about the POC.

P.O.D. stands for the point of destruction:
If in some lifetime you decided, I'm never going to have this amount of money again, because your family got killed for it, or you lost it all and you never wanted to go through that pain again. You have to be destroying you ever since then in order to hold that limitation in place. In order to hold that limitation in place you have to control

your products to not sell that much. You have to control people in not coming to your classes. That's actually because you chose it in another lifetime and you've been destroying all the money you could be generating ever since then.

Everywhere you decided how much money you would never have again, will you destroy and un-create all that?
Right, Wrong, Good, Bad, POC, POD, All 9, Shorts, Boys and Beyonds™.

Shorts stands for:
What's meaningful and meaningless? What are the punishments and rewards? The long version of shorts is: What does _____ mean to us? How do we make it meaningless? What are we punishing ourselves for and torturing ourselves with in relation to it? What are the rewards of it? How many layers and non-layers do we have in relation to it? How much meaningless glop do we have in relation to it?

1. What does <u>having no money</u> mean to you?

You create that positive and negative charge of what money means to you.
Everything that brings up, will you destroy and un-create it all?
Right, Wrong, Good, Bad, POC, POD, All 9, Shorts, Boys and Beyonds™.

2. How do we make <u>having no money</u> meaningless? If we make money meaningful to us and we don't have it, not having money creates pain. To save us from feeling this pain, we are taught to make <u>having no money</u> meaningless by twisting it out of our Universe, as far away from us as possible, so that we don't have to "feel" it. In so doing, we have cut off our awareness as to what is running our life!

Everything that brings up, will you destroy and un-create it all?
Right, Wrong, Good, Bad, POC, POD, All 9, Shorts, Boys and Beyonds™.

3. What are you punishing yourself for and torturing yourself with in relationship to <u>having no money?</u>

Everything that brings up, will you destroy and un-create it all?
Right, Wrong, Good, Bad, POC, POD, All 9, Shorts, Boys and Beyonds™.

4. What are the rewards of <u>having no money</u>? How many layers of crap, or energetic blah do you have in relationship to <u>having no money</u>?

Everything that brings up, will you destroy and un-create it all?
Right, Wrong, Good, Bad, POC, POD, All 9, Shorts, Boys and Beyonds™.

Boys stands for:
Boys refers to anytime you've tried to handle something and it has had no effect. Have you ever done any self-help technique where they told you that you needed to peel the layers of the onion? You kept peeling, and peeling and peeling, and all you got was tears? There are some issues that are onions and some that aren't onions at all. They're called "boys" or nucleated spheres. It's like a kid blowing bubbles on one side of the room and you're on the other side popping bubbles, and the issue never clears.

With "boys" you need to address everywhere you planted the seed of limitation of <u>having no money</u>, somewhere you'd never look to find it. A lot of people work on their money issues. What they do is they take a finance class, an economy class, a math class or make themselves balance their checkbook. You keep trying to pop all these bubbles on the other side of the room when the source of the issue is somewhere else. What you want to do is apply your consciousness to even the places where you've hidden these points of creation of the limitations.

Every nucleated sphere, all the boys that you've created, and all the seeds of limitation that you've planted so deep in your Universe you can't even find them in regards to <u>having no money,</u> will you destroy and un-create all those?
Right, Wrong, Good, Bad, POC, POD, All 9, Shorts, Boys and Beyonds™.

Beyonds stands for:
Have you ever gotten a cell phone bill that was $800 when you thought is was going to be $40? I did. I was talkin' and talkin' and talkin' and all of a sudden I got this bill and went, "Aaaahhhh!" That's the energetic structure called "the beyond." It's anything that basically sends you off into a beyond Universe where you're not present to choose. Does money feel like a beyond for you? The beyonds are all the feelings and sensations. Have you ever looked at your account, and the rent or mortgage is coming up, and you don't know how you're going to eat and your heart races and you start feeling sick? Those are all of the beyonds that are controlling your life.

Everything that brings up and all the feelings, sensations (or beyonds) you have around <u>having no money,</u> will you destroy and un-create all those?
Right, Wrong, Good, Bad, POC, POD, All 9, Shorts, Boys and Beyonds™.

Destroy and Un-Create:
A lot of people hear the word destroy and think, "I don't want to do that." But, what

we're asking you to do is destroy the limitations. If you destroyed all the limitations in your life would that actually be so bad? We use the word un-create, because you are the only one who has created exactly what's showing up in your life right now. You're the only one who has created it, so what we're asking you to do is undo everything you've done to create your life as limited.

SECRET OF THE UNIVERSE: The Clearing Statement
Right, Wrong, Good, Bad, POC, POD, All 9, Shorts, Boys and Beyonds™

Day I ✆ Daily Secret of the Universe

"Your point of view creates your reality; reality doesn't create your point of view."
—Dr. Dain Heer

DAILY EXERCISE: Using "The Clearing Statement" to undo any points of view that aren't working for you.

What if everything you think and everything you say creates absolutely everything that's showing up in your life? What if you're truly a wizard and don't know it? What if you could retrain all your thoughts and everything you say to actually work for you? When I say every point of view you take creates your reality, does that make you feel lighter? If you pay close attention to every thought in your head, you'll discover all of the points of view that are creating your life exactly. When you say or think ... "this is not going to work out" ... you are actually creating the energy of whatever "it" is not working out in your body and life.

One of these points of view might be, "I can't afford this" If you say "I can't afford this," the Universe hears you and un-invites money into your life because it would like to give you everything you're asking for.

Everything that brings up and everywhere you have created "I can't afford this," will you destroy and un-create it all?
Right, Wrong, Good, Bad, POC, POD, All 9, Shorts, Boys and Beyonds™.

After using this clearing statement today, you'll change those points of view and you'll start to experience and receive your life differently.

By doing this, you're going to get better at painting the life you'd actually truly like to have. If you undo all those limited points of view and instead of saying "I can't afford it" say something like "What would it take for the money to show up?" or "I'll have the money, thank you very much, Universe." You've just been handed a new paintbrush and a fresh canvas and you're going to create your life from possibility, choice, and question instead of from limitation. How cool is that?

Day I ❧ Secret of the Universe Written Action Guide

What limiting points of view do you have about money?

❑ _____

❑ _____

❑ _____

❑ _____

❑ _____

❑ _____

**Everything that brings up will you destroy and un-create all of that?
Right, Wrong, Good, Bad, POC, POD, All 9, Shorts, Boys and Beyonds™.**

What limiting points of view do you have about your body?

❑ _____

❑ _____

❑ _____

❑ _____

❑ _____

❑ _____

Everything that brings up will you destroy and un-create all of that?
Right, Wrong, Good, Bad, POC, POD, All 9, Shorts, Boys and Beyonds™.

What limiting points of view do you have about you?

☐ _____

☐ _____

☐ _____

☐ _____

☐ _____

☐ _____

Day I ❧ Secret of the Universe Daily Exercise

For today we're going to begin using "The Clearing Statement" to unravel all the points of view that are not working for you. Pay close attention to every thought in your head and everything you say out loud. Anything that makes you feel heavy run the clearing statement:

Right, Wrong, Good, Bad, POC, POD, All 9, Shorts, Boys and Beyonds™.

STOP . . . experience your daily exercise and come back to the book tomorrow morning. If you're like me, you want "all of you" yesterday. If you stop and use the daily exercise you will begin to integrate these secrets and experience a new life. This will allow you to have a clear foundation to all the secrets of the Universe.

Are you a curious infinite being or what? If you're anything like me you'll get so excited that you'll want to read the entire book cover to cover. This program was created to gift you time to begin playing with these tools in your life and "experience" the changes. If you jump ahead, you'll be robbing you of what you could receive from this program. You can do it. Good job! Close the book and start using your first tool.

Stop . . . See you tomorrow! 🌾

Day 2

Living in and as the question

DAILY EXERCISE: For today, live in and as the question. Take every thought that goes on in your head and turn it into a question.

When you ask a question does it create more possibilities or less? More, right? And when you create any answer does that eliminate all the other possibilities? In the movie *The Matrix* Trinity walks up to Neo and says, "The answer is the question, Neo." What if that were actually true? What if the question was literally the answer that you've been looking for to create everything you desire? What if you could change anything in your life just by asking a question?

How do you receive more money? You ask questions. How does a fabulous, nurturing relationship show up? You ask questions. How do you empower the Universe to gift to you? You ask questions. How do you empower someone to know what's true for them? You ask questions. Questions are your magic wand to creating everything you truly desire. What the question does, is change the energy and begins creating whatever it is that you just asked for. How does it get any easier than that?

We know that "Ask and you shall receive is one of the truths of the Universe," right?

Yet, how many judgments and conclusions do you go to on a daily basis? Everything that brings up will destroy and un-create it all? Right, Wrong, Good, Bad, POC, POD, All 9, Shorts, Boys and Beyonds™.

When you were a kid, how many questions did you ask? Did you ask lots of questions to everyone because you didn't understand why this place was so insane, and why nobody was willing to be joyful or happy? So, you asked, "Why is the sky blue?" "Why do you hate yourself?" "Why are you mean to daddy?" "Why are you mean to yourself?" Basically, all you did was ask questions and wonder what the heck was going on there. And what did your parents do? Did they encourage you to ask questions or did they tell you to be quiet and stop asking questions? In school were we encouraged to ask questions and expand our awareness and knowing? No. We were taught to find the right answer. And if you raised your hand in school and asked a question it meant that you weren't smart enough, or you didn't do your homework, or you didn't know.

Everything that you've done to eliminate your potency of asking questions based on everything you have learned and been taught from this reality, will you destroy and un-create all that?
Right, Wrong, Good, Bad, POC, POD, All 9, Shorts, Boys and Beyonds™.

Every time you ask a question, the Universe is elated and excited to deliver your request. Yet, how many times have you asked a question and then tried to "figure out" how it is going to show up? "How" is not your job! "How" is the Universe's job.

Everything that you've done to try and figure out "how" what you desire, will show up will you destroy and un-create all that?
Right, Wrong, Good, Bad, POC, POD, All 9, Shorts, Boys and Beyonds™.

If you are trying to figure out the answer you are eliminating the infinite ways the Universe can bring you whatever it is you are asking for . . . who do you think is bigger, you or the Universe? Basically when you ask a question and try to go figure it out, you create the conclusions that don't allow the Universe to gift you anything greater. Wouldn't it be easier to allow the Universe to gift to you everything you're asking for?

When you create conclusions, you are basically creating mountains. You then have to climb to overcome all the resistance energy you've created that doesn't allow you to receive what you are asking for.

Another trick to asking questions, is never being vested in the outcome. When you are vested in the outcome is that a move towards question, or a move towards answer? When you live in the question and you have no investment in the outcome, A.K.A. conclusions about "how" anything shows up, everything is really easy and effortless. Everything shows up as if by magic, if you are "being" the question. How do you know that you're asking a question and not vested in the outcome? When you ask questions from that curiosity, from that adventure, and from that wonderment of how this beautiful, contributive Universe is going to support you, literally, it will put together everything showing up as if by magic.

Everything that doesn't allow you to claim, own and acknowledge that the entire Universe is here to totally support you, if all you'd do, was ask questions with no investment in the outcome, will you destroy and un-create all that?
Right, Wrong, Good, Bad, POC, POD, All 9, Shorts, Boys and Beyonds™.

Instead, you can ask and allow every molecule in the entire Universe to gift to you. When you "be" the question you allow the Universe to do all the work for you and your life becomes an adventure, a treasure hunt and a grand and glorious experience. You can wake up every morning with childlike enthusiasm and excitement for your day knowing that the Universe is totally supporting, nurturing, expanding and gifting to your life.

A FEW SECRETS OF THE UNIVERSE ON RECEIVING . . . .

Never choose to be overwhelmed . . . .

How many times have you asked for something to show up in your life, and then when it does, you become overwhelmed by it? If you choose to be overwhelmed, it's literally like telling the Universe . . . I can only handle so much at a time, slow down, only give me a little bit, and the Universe will. It creates confines, that the Universe has to fit into. A little bit limiting, don't you think? Also, being overwhelmed, creates conclusions and judgments which eliminates receiving. Imagine, you have been asking for more business, clients and money to show up. Then it does, and you can't figure out how to have time to do your laundry. You create yourself as overwhelmed by everything you feel you now have "to do". Like going to the bank and depositing all that money. You are telling the Universe . . . "I can handle some business, but total success, is a little bit much." Then the Universe is like . . . okay. Let's give you less, so that you will be happy.

Be out of control with your receiving . . . .

What if you were just receiving so much, that you were so out of control with it, you didn't even have time to create any constructs around it? That way, you could never limit your receiving. For example, you might ask for a million dollars to show up. Then you create all these constructs about how different your life will be and all the things you won't choose anymore and all the things you will choose. This creates all kinds of limitations and judgments, that stops the million dollars from showing up.

Stay away from preferences . . . .

Preferences are giving the Universe the order of what you prefer and when, how, why, and where. "I want more clients like this . . . and less clients like that." That is what will occur. Every preference is actually a conclusion that eliminates receiving. I was driving and thought, "You know, you're doing really well with this Access Consciousness™ work, becoming a big speaker and changing the world; you don't have to be famous as a singer too." As soon as I said that, I caught myself, and ran the clearing statement. If I would have put that in existence it would have killed my singing career, because I am that powerful. Instead, you could just receive everything, and allow yourself to choose in 10 second increments for what works for you in that moment. What if you didn't have any preferences at all and just allowed the Universe to gift you in 10 second increments?

Gratitude creates more receiving . . . .

Every time the Universe gifts you with something and you are grateful for it, and you receive it, you are creating the energy of more receiving. And the more space you be in regards to it, the more the Universe can gift you even more. What if receiving money was like breathing. Do you deserve to breath, or do you just breath? That's the energy we're shooting for in regards to receiving. Gratitude can continue to grow, while satisfaction is a contraction. People think that if they aren't satisfied, they aren't grateful. What if you could be totally grateful and keep asking questions, so that you keep receiving more.

Expand with your receiving . . . .

How many times do you receive and then immediately begin to contract? The more the Universe sees that you are expanded and receiving, the more it can gift to you. Whenever you feel yourself contracting, just expand out and ask, "How does it get any better than this?"

There is no reason to set boundaries . . . .

There are a lot of modalities that teach the importance of setting boundaries. However, does setting boundaries seem like a conclusion or judgment, which eliminates receiving and gifting? Receiving and giving can occur simultaneously. If you allow yourself to choose in 10 second increments you have no need to set boundaries. And if you choose for you, you won't ever feel like a boundary needs to be created. Choosing for you simply means you are in the equation of your choices. And when you choose for you, you are always in gratitude for yourself. You can't have gratitude and judgment in the same Universe. I had no idea that you could choose from the energy of gratitude until I watched my friend do it. She and her good friend, had plans to go for a walk. She was leaving Australia shortly and they were not going to see each other for a few months. That morning her body felt like running with her iPod®. I was present for their phone conversation when she told her friend that she felt like running instead. Most people would have felt "bad" in order to prove that they cared, and created judgments and conclusions about how it was going to upset the other person, and they should have just stuck with the plan. She chose and spoke to her friend from the energy of gratitude and her friend felt honored that she honored herself. When you choose from gratitude for you, it feels like an honoring of the other person as well.

These secrets on receiving, will stop you from stopping you!

HOW DOES IT GET ANY BETTER?

These all apply with receiving with your body as well, the Universe and every molecule that is.

Day 2 ❧ Secret of the Universe Written Exercise

Fill in the Blanks

What would it take for _____ to show up?

What would it take for _____ to show up?

What would it take for _____ to show up?

What would it take for _____ to show up?

What would it take for _____ to turn out better than anything I could have imagined or planned?

What would it take for _____ to turn out better than anything I could have imagined or planned?

What would it take for _____ to turn out better than anything I could have imagined or planned?

What would it take for _____ to turn out better than anything I could have imagined or planned?

What are the infinite ways the Universe could gift me with _____ ?

What are the infinite ways the Universe could gift me with _____ ?

What are the infinite ways the Universe could gift me with _____ ?

What are the infinite ways the Universe could gift me with _____ ?

What would it take for _____ to change with ease, joy and glory?

What would it take for _____ to change with ease, joy and glory?

What would it take for _____ to change with ease, joy and glory?

What would it take for _____ to change with ease, joy and glory?

What generative energy, space and consciousness can me and my body be that would allow _____ to show up?

What generative energy, space and consciousness can me and my body be that would allow _____ to show up?

What generative energy, space and consciousness can me and my body be that would allow _____ to show up?

What generative energy, space and consciousness can me and my body be that would allow _____ to show up?

Here are some more questions to play with...

"How does it get any better than this?"

"What else is possible?"

"What would it take for _____ to show up?"

"What are the infinite possibilities of _____ ?"

"How did I get so lucky this day?"

"What am I unwilling to perceive, know, be, and receive about _____ ?"

"What generative energy, space and consciousness can me and my body be, that would allow for _____ to show up?"

"What grand and glorious adventures with receiving, are me and my body having today?"

"I would choose this, for what reason?"

"Would an infinite being truly choose this?"

"What generative energy, space and consciousness can my body and I be, that would allow us to be the magic we truly be?"

"How could the Universe gift me with more than I am currently willing to receive today?"

"What generative energy, space and consciousness can me and my body be, that would allow us to receive the total invalidation of the limitations of our childhood and our reality?"

"What can I be, do, have, create, generate, institute, choose or change today that would bring me more _____ today and in the future?

If all you did was constantly ask questions . . . could you create any limitation in your life? Or, would your life just "be" an ever-expanding Universe of possibility?

Day 2 ❧ Secret of the Universe Daily Experience

For today, live in and as the question. Make it your experiment. See if you can enjoy the entire day just asking questions. If a conclusion comes up in your head run the clearing statement:

Right, Wrong, Good, Bad, POC, POD, All 9, Shorts, Boys and Beyonds™. Then turn it into a question, so that the Universe can gift you something greater than anything you can currently imagine.

Stop . . . See you tomorrow!

Day 3

What if you are far more psychic and aware then you've ever given yourself credit for?

 DAILY EXERCISE: For today ask, "Who does this belong to?" for every thought, feeling and emotion.

Everything is energy and everything is a vibration. What if you are way more psychic and aware than you've ever given yourself credit for? What if you're like a radio station that is always picking up information from everyone and everything around you at all times? Have you ever thought about someone and they called? Have you finished someone's sentence? That's because you're totally aware.

You are literally like a satellite dish or radio station that is picking up vibrations and frequencies from everything around you. Does it make you feel lighter when I say "98% of the thoughts in your head do not belong to you?" Take a second, does it? Have you ever heard a limited belief or thought in your head and thought, "Who is saying this?" I would never tell myself, "I can't do this." What if none of those limiting thoughts actually belonged to you?

If 98% of your thoughts, feelings, and emotions don't belong to you, how much of your life have you created based on everyone else's point of view? Everything that brings up will you destroy and un-create all that? Right, Wrong, Good, Bad, POC, POD, All 9, Shorts, Boys and Beyonds™.

Imagine a herd of animals. If one senses a predator, what do they do? They all run. They are sending and receiving information and actually know it. Just like we are doing all the time. Only, you think all the thoughts that are going on in your head are all yours. How amazing is that?

What if we all tune our own radio stations? What station would you choose to be tuned into?

Any definition or judgment you have of you or anyone around you, basically tunes the dials to receive more of that information. If you say "I don't have any money," you're tuning you into the station and vibration of those thought-forms and receiving more of that from the world around you. You have defined you as "I don't have money." Therefore, you pick up on those vibrations because they "feel like you."

Everywhere you have tuned your radio station to limited thoughts and judgments that don't work for you, will you destroy and un-create all that? Right, Wrong, Good, Bad, POC, POD, All 9, Shorts, Boys and Beyonds™.

For every thought, every feeling, every emotion and every body pain . . . ask . . . "who does this belong to?" This tool is one of the keys to the kingdom, a doorway to the infinite Universe. Asking "who does this belong to?" will allow you to become a walking meditation. It will create more space and peace in your head and your Universe, and allow you to actually choose for you. It will eliminate eighty-five percent of the pain you think is in your body and get rid of the monkey-mind in your head.

Receiving and using this tool and awareness, is the beginning of the mastery of the creation of being who you would like to be. Because until you know that you are totally aware, you think you are the world around you. Until you know that you are not the world around you, you will be working on everyone's issues thinking it's yours.

Also, by using this tool you are stepping into the aware and potent being you be. This key to the kingdom, allows you freedom, space, and the potential to change and contribute to a new reality for you and the world.

You have been reading minds and energy since before you were born. You just didn't know it. You thought it was you. It wasn't. All you had to do, to receive the freedom and peace of mind, was ask . . . "Who does this belong to?"

This gift of awareness grants you new eyes with which to view the world around you. Now, you are coming from the space of awareness. You are aware of everything around you. Anything that is heavy is not truly you. From this space you can begin choosing what energy you would like to be, instead of always being influenced by the world around you.

After using this tool, a person in one of my classes realized that she had spent $100,000 and thirty years in therapy working on other people's stuff. That's why she never felt like she ever was "healed". She had tried everything under the sun to be free of all this murky energy and it never seemed to completely go away. She had tried yoga, meditation,

Emotional Freedom Technique®, Neuro-Linguistic Programming®, acupuncture, affirmations, you name it, and even though sometimes she felt some clarity and change, something else always came up. She was working on the world around her. After using "Who does this belong to?", she broke out into hysterical laughter because it was never hers to begin with. Instead of feeling riddled with problems that never seemed to go away, asking "Who does this belong to?" allowed her to be the light, energy, space and consciousness she truly is.

Everyone is sending and receiving information all the time. If you think about someone, you are receiving a download from their Universe. If you answer an e-mail, you are receiving a download from their Universe. All you need to do, is be aware that you are sending and receiving information all the time. Do not think it is actually you. Do not resist or align with any energy. Then your awareness of the world around you won't stick to you, and you'll never be affected by it.

What if the Earth is sending and receiving information all the time, too? What if contributing to the Earth was as easy as just asking what she requires, and then being that contribution? Imagine the change we can be, for a new reality.

What if you created your own radio station, and tuned into generative energy, space, and consciousness all the time?

What if you tuned your radio station to Joy? Abundance? Playfulness? Gentleness? What if you are the joy, abundance, playfulness and gentleness you have been looking for? What if all the judgments, conclusions, decisions and heaviness were never yours?

Anything that doesn't allow you to be, know, perceive and receive this, will you destroy and un-create all that now?
Right, Wrong, Good, Bad, POC, POD, Shorts, Boys and Beyonds.

If you were choosing a radio station vibration just for you . . . what would you choose?

If you choose to live from the question and be the space of no judgment, you will find the vibrations of the judgments, conclusions and decisions can't stick you.

Let's do this exercise. Close your eyes. Expand out as big as the city block you are in. Good, now as big as the city . . . the state . . . the country . . . the world . . . the Universe and beyond. Now try to judge . . . You can't, huh? You have to contract yourself in order to go into judgment.

Anytime you feel contracted or limited, you can expand out as big as the Universe. You will not be affected by any limitation from the world around you from this space.

When you are that big, you are tuning into the oneness and consciousness of all things. It's like the radio station of spaciousness, expansiveness and the space of no judgment where you have infinite choice, infinite possibility, and infinite receiving.

Anytime any energy is bombarding you or attempting to control or limit you, expand out as big as the Universe and you will no longer be affected by that energy.

One beautiful being in one of my classes had been keeping herself small, because she thought that if she expanded her being out, she would only pick up even more of the radio station of limitations. What if you are only allowing you to receive 10% of the 1,000% of you that is actually you? She thought she was protecting herself by keeping herself small. In attempting to "protect" herself she was actually cutting off her receiving to the 990% of her and that made her more affected by the 10% of thoughts and judgments from which most people function. After receiving this tool, she became aware that it was exactly the opposite and now she fully receives her expansive being and chooses the radio station that works for her.

If you are tuning your radio station to the limited 10% of you, chances are, you have cut off your awareness. It's okay, because now you have the tools, to know what is you, and what is not, by asking who does this belong to. If you feel trapped or bogged down, you can just expand out. I'm gifting you the keys to the kingdom which are unlocking the doorways to the Universe, day-by-day, tool-by-tool. How does it get any better than this?

All day also remember, "If it's not light as a feather it's not you." This is a great way to become more aware of the energy you truly be. Awareness is light, so light, it's light as a feather. Judgment will always have some sort of "charge" or "polarity" attached to it, while feeling heavy, twisted or dense.

SECRET OF THE UNIVERSE: If it's not light as a feather, it's not you.

Day 3 ❧ Secret of the Universe Daily Exercise

You are about to embark on a three day journey that is one of the biggest secrets of the Universe that most people don't even know exists and almost no one experiences as their awareness.

For the next three days, don't judge any energy and ask, "Who does this belong to?" for every thought, feeling, and emotion. If it gets lighter, it doesn't belong to you. If it gets heavier or sticks around, you just think it's you. Then run the clearing statement . . . .

Everything that makes me think this is me, Right, Wrong, Good, Bad, POC, POD, All 9, Shorts, Boys and Beyonds™.

In addition to the tool, stay expanded out. This tool will be much easier to use if you are as big as the Universe.

Q & A ❧ Questions and Awareness About Today's Exercise

Question: What if I ask "Who does this belong to?" and it doesn't get lighter?

Awareness: You have either defined that vibration as you or you decided it was yours before you asked. Either way run the clearing statement:

Everywhere I decided this was mine I will destroy and un-create all that. Right, Wrong, Good, Bad, POC, POD, All 9, Shorts, Boys and Beyonds™.

If it's still not going away say, "return to sender 10,000-fold with consciousness."

Question: Do you have to know where it comes from?
Awareness: No, you just have to ask.

NOTE: *If you purchased the complete package there are "Who does this belong to?" Post-it® notes. Take a moment right now and "Post-it® note" your house, your car, your computer and everything to remind you for the next three days, "Who does this belong to?"*

Stop . . . See you tomorrow!

Day 4

Having ease with your awareness

DAILY EXERCISE: Today ask, "Who does this belong to?" again for every thought, feeling and emotion. If any point of view sticks, run, "Everything is the opposite of what it appears to be, nothing is the opposite of what it appears to be."

You're going to either love me or hate me for your assignment today, and if you keep going, you will have a whole new life by the end of tomorrow. Does it feel like you are an infinite, spacious, energetic, Superhero being changing all realities? Good! Because by choosing this assignment you actually are choosing to be and receive more!

For today, day four, continue asking the question, "Who does this belong to?" And add . . . .

"Everything is the opposite of what it appears to be, and nothing is the opposite of what it appears to be."

This tool is really awesome when you ask "Who does this belong to?" and it still feels stuck. Running "Everything is the opposite of what it appears to be and nothing is the opposite of what it appears to be" will literally flip anything that is locked in place and shake up the polarity so that it doesn't stick to you. Suddenly, whatever was about to limit you won't even be recalled. How does it get any better or easier than that?

Often you think that your awareness is you, or that you are your awareness. Instead, you are just being aware of the world around you. Until you get that you are not the world around you, you can't begin choosing your life the way you would like to have it.

Remember, if it's not light as a feather, it's not you.

Anytime you receive information that is sticking your Universe with any kind of judgments or conclusions, or radio stations that you aren't choosing for you, just run

"Everything is the opposite of what it appears to be, and nothing is the opposite of what it appears to be."

Have you ever hung out with someone and by the time you left, you felt like they sucked the life out of you? When you feel like any energy is stuck in your body, say over and over "BHCEEMCS everything is the opposite of what it appears to be. BHCEEMCS nothing is the opposite of what it appears to be." Simply run this enough times that you feel laughter or lightness.

This will instantly unlock all of the polarity from you and your body.

BHCEEMCS is your bodies in their entirety. It's your subtle bodies, your energetic bodies, your ethereal bodies as your body in its totality.

Have you ever had the experience of not being able to get someone off your mind? The next time that occurs ask, "Who does this belong to?" Then ask, "Am I thinking about them, or are they thinking about me?" You might find it is they who are thinking of you. They are literally sending you information and you think it is you who are thinking of them. Now that you are aware they are sending you information, return everything to sender ten thousand fold with consciousness. Run everything that is, Right, Wrong, Good, Bad, POC, POD, All 9, Shorts, Boys and Beyonds™. This will allow you to be present to receive your own life, instead of thinking about someone else.

The truth is, we are sending and receiving information all the time. Let's say you have a meeting with someone who wants to invest in your company. After that meeting you're hiking and start thinking about the meeting. Do you think of all the "worst case scenarios?" Guess what, if so, you have just sent the investor back, all of those thoughts which may feel to the investor like thinking of all the reasons why they don't want to invest in your company. Once you've done "Who does this belong to?" for three days and know that nothing belongs to you, you will have a different experience. You will be hiking and receive the awareness that they are thinking about you. At that time the game of "telephone" has begun and the communication lines are open and you can send them back the information you would like them to have. Like, "Oh my, I am so excited to invest in this company. They are going to do so well and make me so much money, etcetera"

All the "worst case scenarios" that you have planted into other peoples Universe's, will you destroy and un-create all that?
Right, Wrong, Good, Bad, POC, POD, All 9, Shorts, Boys and Beyonds™.

Have you ever replayed a conversation with someone over and over in your head?

This can occur because you thought during the conversation that everything they said was true when it wasn't. When this happens there can be a truth with a lie attached either spoken or unspoken. You continue to recall the conversation because you are trying to make a lie true, and the Universe is knocking on your awareness saying "it's not true, it's not true." When this happens, just ask the question "What is the truth here, and what is the lie?" Once you allow yourself to receive the truth that something they said was a lie everything will get lighter and that conversation will stop playing in your head.

This key to the kingdom is very powerful with so-called "psychic attacks". Sometimes you are being a very potent and expansive being and others are throwing little daggers into your Universe because they are unsettled with the limited reality they are choosing. Cool, all that is required is for you to run . . . "everything is the opposite of what it appears to be, and nothing is the opposite of what it appears to be." This literally changes all the judgments you might have of you, and shakes up your vibration so you can't be located. People locate you based on your judgments of you.

I use the word "potency" instead of "power" because in this reality "power" usually means "power over others." Potency reads more energetically correct because you are already potent and have diluted that potency in order to take on any limitations.

Okay, let's talk for a second about your mind. Your mind can only confine and define what you already know. If your thinking mind had all the answers to your life, wouldn't you have everything figured out by now? Also, how much has your thinking mind eliminated you receiving? Have you ever gotten a massage and thought the whole time then run thought, "Why did I just pay for that? I didn't receive at all." Also what is the difference between thinking and knowing? When you know, you don't have to think about it. You just know. How much has your thinking mind talked you out of your knowing? Have you ever known you shouldn't have gotten into a relationship, and then talked yourself into it and it turned out just the way you knew it was going to? What I like to say is "If you're thinking, you're stinking."
How much has your thinking mind run your life?
Spoiled your fun?

Limited your receiving?

What if you could choose to be totally present, totally receiving all the time?
These tools are the keys to the kingdom because they give you everything that is required so that you can be the generative energy, space and consciousness you truly be.

What if you continue asking "who does this belong to?" and running "Everything is the opposite of what it appears to be and nothing is the opposite of what it appears to be" for any energy especially the heavy stuff that comes into your Universe? Then you can be free to choose.

If you could choose anything, and everything was possible, what would you choose?

Day 4 ❧ Secret of the Universe Daily Exercise

For today also ask this question "Who does this belong to?" for every thought, feeling, and emotion. If it gets lighter, it doesn't belong to you. If it gets heavier or sticks around, you just think it's you. Then run the clearing statement . . . Everything that brings up, Right, Wrong, Good, Bad, POC, POD, All 9, Shorts, Boys and Beyonds™.

Today also add the tool "Everything is the opposite of what it appears to be. Nothing is the opposite of what it appears to be."

Q & A ❧ Questions and Awareness About Today's Exercise

Question: Do I have to say it out load?
Awareness: No, it works if you say it in your head, too.

NOTES: _____

_____

_____

_____

_____

_____

Stop . . . See you tomorrow!

Day 5

Having ease with your body's awareness

DAILY EXERCISE: For the third day ask, "Who does this belong to?" again for every thought, feeling and emotion. Also, if you're aware of someone's body or Universe and it feels like it's sticking to your body run "BHCEEMCS, everything is the opposite of what it appears to be, BHCEEMCS, nothing is the opposite of what it appears to be." Also add, "Body, Thank you so much for this awareness. You don't have to take this on. It's okay, they are choosing it because they love it. Will you let them keep it?"

Our bodies are infinite space. Quantum physics states that we are ninety-nine percent space and seventy percent water. The distance between the atom of one molecule and the outside edge is the distance between the earth to the sun. So, if you're 99% space and 70% water, that's not malleable and changeable based on what? Based on your point of view.

Have you bought points of view from science stating that bodies are matter and more dense, and can't be space? Everywhere you have bought all of those points of view from science will you destroy and un-create all of that?
Right, Wrong, Good, Bad, POC, POD, All 9, Shorts, Boys and Beyonds™.

A lot of people think that judgment and conclusion is somehow the creation of their body. What if every judgment and conclusion that you went to, was actually a "little death" for your body? When you judge or conclude do you feel expansive or contractive? Contractive, right?

Anywhere you think judgment or conclusion will create any generative energy in your body instead of just destroy it, will you destroy and un-create all that?
Right, Wrong, Good, Bad, POC, POD, All 9, Shorts, Boys and Beyonds™.

Science tells us that our cells are spherical. When a thought intersects with those molecules they become oblong, which is the basis for the creation of aging, disease and disorder. When you were a little kid all of your molecules were round and beautiful and vibrant! They were like "Superhero" molecules.

You impact your molecules with the definition of you, all the judgments "you" think "you" are, everything you resist, and everything with which you align with. You are the one who tells your molecules to begin to be oblong and to start creating the death, disease and destruction that you think is eminent.

Everywhere you feel like the death and destruction of the body is eminent and that's just the way it is, will you destroy and un-create it all?
Right, Wrong, Good, Bad, POC, POD, All 9, Shorts, Boys and Beyonds™.

What if every molecule in the entire Universe functions from question and is completely generative? If you spray "Round Up®" on a weed, the molecules of the weed begin to ask how they can change and transform to "be the question" that allows them to transform and survive. Eventually, the weeds transform and become immune to that particular formula of "Round up®". Then a new version of the weed killer has to be created to try and kill the new weeds, and again the molecules go into question and beat the formula.

Everything you are doing to create your body as not totally generative, will you destroy and un-create it all?
Right, Wrong, Good, Bad, POC, POD, All 9, Shorts, Boys and Beyonds™.

Having Ease with Your Body's Awareness . . . .

What if your body really is more conscious than you are?

Your body is a sensory organ. It is here to give you information. Have you ever sat down next to someone and started thinking, "I think I'm getting a headache?" Later you hear them talking about their splitting headache and think "Wait a minute! I thought headaches weren't contagious!" The way to begin having ease with your body's awareness is, first, never say "I feel", always say "I'm perceiving." What's the difference between feeling and perceiving? When you say "I feel" now you've aligned with it, and it will take longer to undo the energy because your point of view creates your reality. If you say "I'm perceiving this" and have no point of view about it, the energy will disappear as quickly as it came.

Every time you "think" you feel tired, sick, or some pain, could it be your body is just giving you information about the world around you? If you take a point of view about your awareness, like "I'm tired" then you will lock that energy into your body and reality.

One of the ways to not lock other peoples' energies into your body is talking to your body like you would a little child, and thanking it for all the information it is giving you. "Thank you, my awesome body, for all that information. It's okay. You don't have to take it on. Is there anything you require from me right now? What generative energy, space and consciousness can I be for you right now?" You and your body can be a contribution and source of energy for each other.

What if part of conscious embodiment is being grateful and adoring your body as if it's your best friend and your lover?

You wake up so happy to be together you tell it over and over just how much you adore and love it. There really isn't anything you wouldn't do for it. You caress it, sing to it, thank it, praise it, adore it, listen to it, care for it, honor it, and choose for its happiness and well being. Imagine how much energy in your life you could shift by befriending your body in its entirety. Imagine all the happy, blissful, bodies walking around, in communion with the entire Universe.

Day 5 ❧ Secret of the Universe Daily Exercise

For the third day ask this question "Who does this belong to?" for every thought, feeling, and emotion. If it gets lighter, it doesn't belong to you. If it gets heavier or sticks around, you just think it's you. Then run the clearing statement . . . Everything that brings up, Right, Wrong, Good, Bad, POC, POD, All 9, Shorts, Boys and Beyonds™.

1. In addition to the tool for bodies add, "BHCEEMCS, everything is the opposite of what it appears to be. BHCEMMCS, nothing is the opposite of what it appears to be."

2. In addition to those tools for bodies "Body, thank you so much for this awareness. You don't have to take this on. It's okay. They are choosing it because they love it. Will you let them keep it?"

SECRET OF THE UNIVERSE: Never say, "I feel" always say, "I perceive."

Stop . . . See you tomorrow!

Day 6

Getting Out of Judgment

DAILY EXERCISE: For today every time you're about to judge yourself, picture a stop sign, then run, Everything that brings up, Right, Wrong, Good, Bad, POC, POD, All 9, Shorts, Boys and Beyonds™. Then choose a generative energy of what you love about you or your body.

What does judgment actually do?

1. Creates more judgments.

2. Influences the way you see and receive the world. (judgment goggles)

3. Eliminates receiving.

4. Locks whatever you're judging in place.

5. Creates separation.

6. Creates your experience.

7. Cuts off your awareness.

Does judgment ever make you feel lighter? Since we know the truth will make you feel lighter and a lie will make you feel heavier, what if all judgment was basically a lie? Below is an explanation of what judgment really does.

1. Judgment creates more judgments. Judgment is like a multi-level marketing scheme of limitation. In order to hold a judgment in place you have to hold at least five other judgments in place. In order to hold those judgments in place, you have to hold five other judgments in place. It's like creating a spider web of illusion and lies that are all connected and keep you trapped in your judgment. We call this "*The Kingdom of Crapdom.*"

For example:

- Judgment #1 — If you judge your thighs as being fat.
- Judgment #2 — You have to judge what thin thighs would look like.
- Judgment #3 — What fat thighs would look like.
- Judgment #4 — What that means about you and your body.
- Judgment #5 — How others view your fat thighs.
- Judgment #6 — You'll probably judge other peoples' thighs.
- Judgment #7 — You may also eliminate receiving other things based on your judgment of your thighs. For example; That you don't deserve a nurturing relationship or great sex because of your fat thighs.
- Judgment #8 — How your life would be better if you had thin thighs . . . etcetera, etcetera, etcetera.

- **Judgment influences the way you see and receive the world (judgment goggles).** In regards to you having a judgment about your thighs, you'll also find yourself haunted by judging other peoples' thighs. Any judgment you have of you or your body, you project those judgments onto the world and see everything through those judgments. Ever judged what kind of a car you wanted to buy, and from that point forward did you then notice that car everywhere? You do that same thing with every judgment you have of you and your body.

  Guess what else? Every judgment you have of you or your body, you are tuning your radio station to pick up on those judgments from the "collective unconscious." If you have a judgment that you have "fat thighs" have you ever noticed that you never hear in your head, "my thighs are so skinny?" Nope. That's because that particular thought pattern doesn't feel like "you."

- **Judgment eliminates receiving.** If someone came into your life and really loved your thighs, thought they were ultra sexy, you would be unable to receive them loving your thighs, and make them wrong because you already judged the "truth," from your point of view, about your own thighs.

  Have you ever been having sex with someone and you're making out, passionately, your bodies are tingling and the chemistry is hot? During that, have you ever gone into some sort of judgment of you, your body, them, their body, some smell or look and had the energy stop? That's what judgment does. It eliminates receiving.

  Also, people will judge you in order to not receive you. If you are being any energy they are not willing to be people will create judgments in order to not receive from you.

Like, if you are being super sexy and receiving your body and life as an orgasmic experience, anyone that doesn't allow themselves to receive that will judge you. They have to create the judgments in order to not receive that energy. They judge in order to validate their reality of not receiving.

What if every judgment you received made you $5,000 that year. Next time someone judges you say in your head . . . "Cha-ching!"

Still unwilling to receive judgment? What if any judgment someone had meant nothing to you, and just gave you more information about how they judge themselves?

Also, if people start judging you, the trick is to get bigger and wilder. People judge in order to control you. When you are unaffected, they will stop judging you because their judgments aren't working.

• **Judgment also locks what you are judging into place.** If you judge "My thighs are fat." You're telling your molecules, "Thank you very much, I would like fat thighs." By every judgment of what you've decided is "wrong" with you or your life, you are locking those areas in place instead of asking a question to unlock them. Asking a question is a move toward unlocking the energy. Judgment is a move toward locking it in place.

• **Judgment creates separation.** Have you ever judged a friend? After you judged them did you feel closer to them or more separate from them? The truth always feels light, and a lie heavy. Awareness is always light as a feather, and a judgment feels heavy. Remember, "If it's not light as a feather, it's not you!"

Can you imagine if the sun chose not to shine because it was having a bad "hair day?" Or the birds chose not to sing because they thought they didn't sing well enough? Or dolphins wouldn't jump and play in the ocean because they thought they were fat?

The density and polarity of the world of judgments has no right to take your fun away, or stop you from playing, loving, adoring, and living your phenomenal life.

• **Judgments create your experience.** At one time I used to have a terrible reaction to people who were smoking pot. Anytime anyone was stoned around me I would feel like my lungs were being stabbed, my throat would close up and my head would spin, almost like a panic attack. One day I was walking in Hawaii with a fellow Access Consciousness™ facilitator friend and saw people smoking pot across the park. I began to react to this energy and started doing everything I could to not be affected. I quickly tried to put up walls and barriers, ignore it, cut off my awareness to it (I call this *Ninjitsu of Not Receiving*) and anything I could think of to not be affected. The facilitator that was with me asked, "What are you doing?" At that moment I heard the founder of Access Consciousness™ Gary Douglas say, "Your point of view creates your reality, reality doesn't create your point of view." And I thought, "Hold on, what points of view and judgments do I have here?" I realized my judgments were creating this terrible experience. For the next 30 minutes we ran clearing statements on all the judgments I had about smoking pot and other people smoking pot until I had no point of view about it. Now I can be around people who smoke pot and it has no "effect" on me. I went from totally affected to having no effect in my body.

So every energy that you've judged as "negative" which is creating a negative experience, will you destroy and un-create all that?
Right, Wrong, Good, Bad, POC, POD, All 9, Shorts, Boys and Beyonds™.

• **Judgment also cuts off your awareness** because anything that doesn't match that judgment can't come into your Universe. Have you ever judged that someone was "perfect" for you? How long did it take you to become aware of who that person really was? Ever said, "Oh my God! I thought I knew you. I can't believe you did this to me!" What occurred there is that you created positive judgments about them, like "they are kind and caring," "they would never do that to me," "they would never lie to me." Those judgments cut off your awareness and from that point forward you couldn't be aware of them doing any of that.

Everything that brings up, will you destroy and un-create all that?
Right, Wrong, Good, Bad, POC, POD, All 9, Shorts, Boys and Beyonds™.

All judgment creates more limitation. Did you know even the so-called "positive" judgments you have of yourself and body can create limitation, too?

For example, if you judge yourself to be a kind and caring person, that can create a limitation in your Universe because you will be unwilling to be any other energy. I thought if someone accuses you of not being a kind and caring person you will do anything to prove that you are. Then they can literally control, manipulate, and dominate you by this positive judgment you have of yourself.

If you have judged yourself to be kind and caring, then anytime someone throws into your Universe that you aren't, you will choose to prove to them you are. You will agree to do something for them, instead of choose for you, because that is what kind and caring people do.

Anywhere you have defined you to be or not be any energy, will you destroy and un-create that now?
Right, Wrong, Good, Bad, POC, POD, All 9, Shorts, Boys and Beyonds™.

Also, anytime you are proving anything, you actually believe the opposite. Somewhere, behind this judgment of kind and caring, you believe that you are not kind and caring at all. It creates a hot button for everyone to push.

The truth is, you are an infinite being and you can choose to be any energy at will and choice. Next time someone accuses you of something like "you're manipulative" you can say, "Thank you, I can be that!" The truth is you are everything; kind, caring, mean, sad, joyful and everything else. You have access to "be" any energy that you choose to be.

The keys to the kingdom: Unlocking the doorways to the Universe.

What if you stopped judging you today?

I had this amazing, light, very potent being in class, who has been judging herself to be a kind, compassionate and caring person. Which was a part of all the energy she embodied. Yet, because she was holding this judgment of her in place, she was always playing the "Miss Nice, Miss Nice" role and allowing others to totally manipulate, dominate and control her. If someone wanted something from her, all they would need to do is pretend that they needed her help, and she couldn't say no because that didn't fit with her role of being a nice person. But, eventually, she would get so tired of not choosing for her, she would explode and then eliminate these people from her life. We ran some clearings of judgments with her, and opened up her awareness of the full potency she be. Now she breezes through her interactions and chooses for her, without judgment and receives more of everything.

And yes, my friend, it is that easy.

Guess what else? When others judge you, they are just trying to control you. If you don't judge yourself, they will have nothing with which to control you. You will receive their judgments like you receive the rain. They will go right through you. They will have a hard time remembering what they were judging about you.

People will judge you to not receive the energy they are unwilling to be. If you are being an energy that someone is not willing to be, they will of necessity judge you in order to create separation and not receive that energy. If you are being yummy sexualness and they are not willing to be it, they will judge "Oh, my god! they're so sexual, I would never be that!" Because, if they didn't judge you, they would receive that sexualness and it would undo their judgments of themselves.

47

- What if you are not wrong?
- What if you've never been wrong?
- What if nothing you've ever said or ever done has been wrong, ever?
- What if there is nothing judge-able about you?

  What if there never has been . . . .

LIST SOME JUDGMENTS YOU HAVE OF YOUR BODY

❑ _____

❑ _____

❑ _____

❑ _____

❑ _____

❑ _____

❑ _____

Will you destroy and un-create everything that brings up?
Right, Wrong, Good, Bad, POC, POD, All 9, Shorts, Boys and Beyonds™.

LIST SOME THINGS YOU ARE GRATEFUL ABOUT YOUR BODY . . . .

❑ _____

❑ _____

❑ _____

❑ _____

❑ _____

❑ _____

❑ _____

LIST SOME JUDGMENTS YOU HAVE OF YOU . . . .

- ☐ _____
- ☐ _____
- ☐ _____
- ☐ _____
- ☐ _____
- ☐ _____
- ☐ _____
- ☐ _____

Will you destroy and un-create everything that brings up?
Right, Wrong, Good, Bad, POC, POD, All 9, Shorts, Boys and Beyonds™.

LIST SOME THINGS YOU LOVE ABOUT YOU . . . .

- ☐ _____
- ☐ _____
- ☐ _____
- ☐ _____
- ☐ _____
- ☐ _____
- ☐ _____
- ☐ _____
- ☐ _____

Day 6 ∞ Secret of the Universe Daily Exercise

Getting out of judgment. For today, every time you're about to judge yourself picture a stop sign, then run, Everything that brings up, Right, Wrong, Good, Bad, POC, POD, All 9, Shorts, Boys and Beyonds™. Then choose a generative energy of what you love about you or your body.

Here's how it works: If you're about to judge your wrinkles, picture a stop sign. Run the clearing statement. Then choose a generative energy like "my beautiful eyes, I love my eyes."

If you're about to judge a friend, picture a stop sign. Then ask, "What am I grateful for here?"

ANOTHER SECRET NOTE ∞ If 98% of your thoughts, feelings and emotions don't belong to you, do you suppose 98% of your judgments don't belong to you too? If you haven't done "Who does this belong to?" for three days, go back and do that before you go on. Because, literally, you might spend the rest of the program working on issues that never belonged to you.

Also, there hasn't been anything you haven't been or done in some lifetime, so if you find yourself going into judgment of someone else, . . . first ask, "Is this my judgment of them or their judgment of themselves?" Whichever feels lighter is true. People wear their judgments like neon signs and you read them. If you find that you are the one creating the judgments, . . . there isn't anything that you haven't been or done in some lifetime and still have judgments of you in this area. If so, then run, "Destroy and un-create everywhere I've been there or done this in any lifetime." Right, Wrong, Good, Bad, POC, POD, All 9, Shorts, Boys and Beyonds™.

NOTES: _____

_____

_____

_____

_____

Stop . . . See you tomorrow! 🌾

Day 7

What if you lost your capacity to judge?

Daily Exercise:
Step 1: Strip down in front of the mirror totally naked and look at your body.
Step 2: Notice where you contract or judge.
Step 3: Then destroy and un-create everything you have resisted and reacted to or aligned and agreed with and allows that judgment to exist. Right, Wrong, Good, Bad, POC, POD, All 9, Shorts, Boys and Beyonds™.
Do steps 1-3 until you look in the mirror and can't find anything to judge, as if you are looking at a beautiful plant or orchid and are in adoration of every curve, every shape, every color and texture.

What if there is nothing judge-able about you or your body . . . .
What if you lost your capacity to judge?

Have you used the mirror as a way to unleash a litany of judgment onto you? When you look in a mirror, do you use this as an opportunity to locate and judge everything that is wrong about your body? Do you judge your skin, your weight, your aging, your hair, everything? Or, do you look into a mirror and receive the amazing, beautiful being you be?

Everything that brings up, will you destroy and un-create it all?
Right, Wrong, Good, Bad, POC, POD, All 9, Shorts, Boys, and Beyonds.

What you see in the mirror is a culmination of your judgments. Everything you have judged and decided about your body, will jump out at you every time you look in the mirror. It's like when you decide you want to buy a new car and everywhere you go you see that car.

What if you actually began creating the space of caring and gratitude for your body? Every time you walked in front of a mirror that caring is what you received.

What if the mirror actually became your friend, because your awareness of you was that you are a beautiful and gorgeous being? What if you used mirrors for you, instead of against you, and every time you looked in the mirror you saw how beautiful you truly are?

Because, surprise, you really are.

Now, if you look into the mirror and think, "I'm so beautiful," but your point of view is, "I'm ugly," you won't be able to step into the awareness of your beauty. That's why affirmations don't work. You have to undo the electrical charge of your underlying point of view to actually step into the space of awareness of your beautiful body. Remember the difference between awareness and judgment is that awareness is light and judgment has a "charge" to it.

If you think that your judgments are true and real, you will never allow yourself to be or receive the energy that will create the change.

The first step to changing anything in regards to your body or life is to get out of judgment. Whenever you judge anything, you are locking that energy in place instead of asking the question that would change it.

• What have you decided is wrong about you, your body and your life?
• Is that a move to unlock it? Or lock it in place?

Everything that brings up, will you destroy and un-create it all?
Right, Wrong, Good, Bad, POC, POD, All 9, Shorts, Boys, and Beyonds

From the space of no judgment you could choose to be the energy that changes your body. The space of no judgment is the total adoration for everything that it is, just the way it is. Then you can begin being the question that leads to a greater possibility.

In one of my private sessions, a woman shared with me that someone came up to her and said, "I know someone who has a great cream for your red face." It wasn't said maliciously, but that night she went home and her face turned bright red. She was really angry and upset. When she came into her private session with me the next day she said, "What do I do? I know when people tell me stuff and it's a lie, I just POC and POD it and move on. But what about when it's true?"

I just started laughing! So, I asked, "What did somebody tell you that is true?" The woman said, "she told me she had some cream for my red face!" I asked, "Is that true or is that a judgment?"

She thought that judgment was actually true, instead of just someone's judgment. We know from the last chapter that judgments create more of what you're judging, so her body became inflamed because it wanted to show her that she bought that judgment as true. Since she had the awareness of that judgment not being true, her face isn't red at all and she also lost fifteen pounds!

Once you are being that space of caring for every molecule to be exactly what it is, you can begin to change your body. Here are some examples of how to communicate with the molecules of your body. If you were asking a plant to grow another flower for you to adore . . . what energy would you be? More like, "Hey babe, let me flow you some energy, come on out." Is there a need or necessity in the plant to grow another flower for you? No. You don't say to the plant, "If you don't grow, I'm going to make you wrong." If you wake up every day and say, "Yes! Look at how beautiful you are! I'm not making you do anything, I'm just asking, What else is possible? Be excited to receive it. If you wanted a dog to know how much you cared for it, what energy would you be? What if you began communicating with your body from the generative energies of gratitude, adoration and receiving?

Be aware of every time you think; this is stupid, make believe or not real, because those are the thoughts you want to POC and POD. This is where you think your judgments of your body are real.

Think back to a time when you had a visit at the doctor's office. Do most doctor's go into any question at all? Or, do they just give you a conclusion of what is wrong or right with your body. Did you agree as if it was true and unchangeable? Or, did you resist and react? If you resisted or reacted to it, you locked that energetic pattern in place.

Everything that brings up, will you destroy and un-create it all?
Right, Wrong, Good, Bad, POC, POD, All 9, Shorts, Boys, and Beyonds

Once you feel that space of no judgment in your Universe and have total caring for every molecule, as if you were looking at a beautiful orchid plant, you won't be able to find anything to judge. Once you begin perceiving that space, you can begin asking your body for whatever it is you would like your body to be or look like.

• If you were asking a plant to grow another flower for you, what energy would that be?

• If you were talking to a dog, to let it know you cared about it, what energy would you be?

Loving, nurturing? More like talking to the seeds in the ground encouraging them to grow, and then being that nurturing energy for them, without judgment. You are not going to get mad and be mean if it doesn't grow. When you are talking to the dog, are you looking at the tail and thinking it's too long, or too short and now you don't like it?

You are just being the space of what else is possible, and receiving what else is possible.

Day 7 *Secret of the Universe Daily Experience*

STEP 1: Strip down in front of the mirror totally naked and look at your body.

STEP 2: Notice where you contract or judge.

STEP 3: Then destroy and un-create everything you have resisted and reacted to, or aligned and agreed with that allows that judgment to exist. Right, Wrong, Good, Bad, POC, POD, All 9, Shorts, Boys and Beyonds™.

Do steps 1-3 until you look in the mirror and can't find anything to judge. It's as if you are looking at a beautiful plant or orchid and are in adoration of every curve, every shape, every color and texture.

• What would it be like to step into the space of no judgment and into the space of caring?

• What would it be like to unravel all the judgments . . . so you can be free to be and receive?

NOTES: _____

_____

_____

_____

_____

Stop . . . See you tomorrow!

Day 8

Your body is your greatest conscious facilitator

DAILY EXERCISE: Being conscious with food.
STEP 1: Muscle test every bite of food you eat today.
STEP 2: Destroy and un-create all the decisions, judgments, computations and conclusions you have about the food you're muscle testing. Right, Wrong, Good, Bad, POC, POD, All 9, Shorts, Boys and Beyonds™.
STEP 3: Muscle test again. You may be surprised that the "answer" or awareness your body gives you, after you let go of all of your points of view, changes.

What if your body is more conscious than you are? What if your body could be your greatest conscious facilitator? What if you asked your body, "Hey body, what do you know about changing this?" What if it would actually gift you the energy that would create the change? If you still have judgments about your body, you can't have that clear communion and can't create change.

What if you began honoring your body and asking it questions for everything that involves it? Do you eat or does your body eat? Your body eats. Do you have sex or does your body have sex? Your body has sex.

- What if you asked your body how long "it" wanted to live . . . .

- "Body, how long would you choose to live?"

- One hundred years or more?

- Two hundred years or more?

- Three hundred years or more?

- Four hundred, five hundred, six hundred?

- More?

- How much judgment and conclusion do you go to on a daily basis in order to kill yourself in the appropriate time period?

What if anytime you contract you create a little death in your body? Your point of view creates your reality, so we basically tell our molecules with our judgments and conclusions to get old and die. Do you have a point of view about what you will look like when you're 40? 50? 60? 70? 80? 90? Or 100? Or are you already dead at 100? Since your point of view creates your reality, every one of those points of view creates exactly that.

Everything that brings up, will you destroy and un-create it all?
Right, Wrong, Good, Bad, POC, POD, All 9, Shorts, Boys, and Beyonds.

• What if judgment is actually the most toxic thing there is?

Our bodies are as big as our physical structure. We as beings are as big as the Universe. When you stay as expanded as the Universe, you can receive all that energy for your body.

• What if what you see in the mirror every day was a culmination of your judgments?

• Wrinkles, stored fat, everything?

Everywhere you have been trying to lose weight, when what is really required is losing the judgments, will you destroy and un-create all that?
Right, Wrong, Good, Bad, POC, POD, All 9, Shorts, Boys, and Beyonds.

• What if you began being in communion with your body?

In order to change anything that is going on in your body . . . .
STEP 1: Stop judging your body.
STEP 2: Destroy and Un-create all your judgments and conclusions.
STEP 3: Ask it what it would take to change.
STEP 4: Listen to what it requires for that change to occur.

In the beginning of creating a clear connection with your body, you're going to muscle test everything that has to do with your body.

All you need to do is put your feet together and hold whatever it is in front of your solar plexus, and just ask your body . . . body do you require this?
If your body falls forward, it is a yes. If your body falls backwards, it's a no.

What if everything was that easy? Having no point of view, asking, and listening. If you have a point of view about what you are muscle testing, your body will muscle test that same point of view.

If you judge that Coke® is "bad," your body will muscle test a "no" in regards to Coke®. If you undo all your points of view you might be surprised what occurs.

How much do you overeat or judge to cut off your awareness, or dull yourself to this reality, so you can fit in? Have you ever overeaten at a family function? Do you suppose it's because you wanted to "fit in?" So, you "cut off your awareness" to "be like them" to be as little energy as possible, so you aren't "too much?"

Everything that brings up, will you destroy and un-create it all?
Right, Wrong, Good, Bad, POC, POD, All 9, Shorts, Boys, and Beyonds.

How much do you overeat in order to not be and receive the sexualness you truly be?
Everything that brings up, will you destroy and un-create it all?
Right, Wrong, Good, Bad, POC, POD, All 9, Shorts, Boys, and Beyonds.

How many of you have duplicated your parents' reality and made your bodies look like them? Everything that brings up, will you destroy and un-create it all?
Right, Wrong, Good, Bad, POC, POD, All 9, Shorts, Boys, and Beyonds.

• What if the biggest form of abuse is not allowing your body to choose for itself?

What would it be like if you were conscious with the food you ate? What if you allowed your body to choose everything that has to do with it? For today, our exercise is muscle test and be conscious with every bite of food. For every bite, taste the flavors exploding on your tongue. Notice how the different taste buds are activated and how it feels to have the different textures exploding in your mouth. Invite and receive the orgasmic energy eating consciously can be. Every bite of food should taste orgasmic. If not, POC and POD your judgments about the food, if it still doesn't taste orgasmic, stop eating it. Your body is done.

When you actually receive the orgasmic energy for your body, it's a generative energy for your body. The energy of orgasm is the energy of creation and generation, of a generative body. Your molecules "wake up" and are excited to receive and taste. What if you allowed your body to communicate with you about what "it" requires and desires?

Day 8 ❧ Secret of the Universe Daily Exercise

BEING CONSCIOUS WITH THE FOOD YOU EAT.

STEP 1: Muscle test every bite of food you eat today.

STEP 2: Destroy and un-create all the decisions, judgments, computations and conclusions you have about the food you're muscle testing. Right, Wrong, Good, Bad, POC, POD, All 9, Shorts, Boys and Beyonds™.

STEP 3: Muscle test again. You may be surprised that the answer or awareness your body gives, you after you let go of all of your points, of view changes.

NOTES: _____

_____

_____

_____

_____

_____

_____

_____

_____

_____

_____

_____

_____

Stop . . . See you tomorrow!

Day 9

Getting out of the wrongness of you —you are an alien

DAILY EXERCISE:
After reading today's chapter, experience your life, body and the planet through your new and different eyes. Then journal the unveiling of your magical adventurous day.

Imagine you are an alien, that is just about to choose a body and family here on this earth, and everything is completely foreign to you . . . .

You are in your spaceship looking at this whole "matrix of reality," thinking, "Wow, that's interesting. Huh, they must not know what is possible. They believe they have all these problems and are always making themselves wrong. None of this is mandatory, and all of it is not true and not real. That's strange! They judge themselves and love feeling terrible about their lives. With their choice of creating these judgments and conclusions, they eliminate almost all of their capacity to receive. This is so weird! How does this work? Why would anyone choose this? Surely, if they knew what was actually possible, they wouldn't make these choices. All I have to do is be the generative energy, space and consciousness, no judgment and infinite caring I be, and it will undo all the limitation from which they think they are suffering and allow them to receive a living that is greater than anything they can currently imagine! These people are going to love me! I'm ready. Let's embody! This is going to be fun and easy!"

You jump into your mother's womb excited for all the change and possibility that she and everyone else is going to receive . . . .

And what happens next? You begin creating a body in her sweet little tummy and being this gift that would undo everything she believes is wrong about her and what does she do? Does she receive you? Or does she do everything else BUT receive you? She judges and concludes about everything and you wonder, what the heck is going on here?

There's one more caveat that I forgot to mention. When you embodied, you forgot that there was a difference between you and her, so you think you're the one thinking all of her thoughts. Here are some of the ramblings that she may have thought that you think you are the one thinking . . . .

"I'm not sure if I want this baby, it's going to be a lot of work. God, I'm going to be a bad mother. Maybe I should have gotten an abortion. I can't believe I thought that! I'm a terrible person! God, I hate my body! I'm so fat! My husband and I haven't had sex in months. I bet he thinks I'm unattractive. Of course he thinks I'm unattractive! I'm huge! He doesn't want to touch me! Maybe he's found someone else, younger and prettier. My body will never be the same!"

How many thoughts did you buy as yours and create your reality from while you were in your mother's womb? How much of that has influenced the relationship between you and your father?
Everything that brings up, will you destroy and un-create all that?
Right, Wrong, Good, Bad, All 9, POC, POD, Shorts, Boys and Beyonds.

You might think, "Maybe they just need to see my cute cherub-like face to receive the gift I am. Once I'm born, then they'll receive me." So, you go through the birthing process, which is quite energetically challenging for you as most moms are in pain, and cursing your delivery.

Everywhere you think you being born was a burden, will you destroy and un-create all that?
Right, Wrong, Good, Bad, All 9, POC, POD, Shorts, Boys and Beyonds.

Then, you were born, show your little cherub face and think, "Ahhh . . . I'm here, now you can let go of all of your limitations and we can change everything."

What happens? Does everyone around receive the gift of infinite caring and joy you be that unravels all limitation? What, they didn't? I guess your parents did exactly what mine did. They begin creating judgments, projections, rejections, expectations, and conclusions about you and your life and what you will be for them. You look like your mother. You have your father's nose. I hope you don't go bald by forty, like grandpa . . . etcetera.

All of the projections, rejections, expectations, judgments, and conclusions that were delivered at you in the womb or through your childhood, will you destroy and un-create all that?
Right, Wrong, Good, Bad, All 9, POC, POD, Shorts, Boys and Beyonds.

Yet, you are still this little "alien" of infinite space, caring and gratitude. Think of a little newborn baby. Isn't it kind of hard to judge a baby?

Still, you are judged and not received almost every 10 seconds of your new life on this planet. You think enthusiastically, "That's okay if they don't receive me. I'm a gift. I know I am." Like the little engine that could . . . "Maybe they just need more time." So you wait, and be the infinite space, caring and gratitude, and think, "They'll receive me. I know they will." Yet what do they do? This occurs over and over again until you begin to think, "I must not work. Me, as a being, doesn't work. I must be wrong, because they aren't receiving me. Maybe, if I can just understand what they are doing, then it won't hurt so much to be here." From that point forward, you are stuck attempting to understand the "insane asylum" called "this reality." Not only that, in order for them to not receive you, they must go into judgment. Here's how it goes . . . you be you (the energy, space and consciousness that unravels all limitation), and they judge themselves or you, which is really contractive and mean to themselves. After that happens a few billion times, are you going to think, that you being you, actually creates pain? So, you stop being you, and think that you, as a being, must be wrong.

Since you feel so deeply wrong for being, you then try to prove how right you are. Which locks you into the matrix of this reality.
Everything that you've made wrong about you, will you destroy and un-create it all?
Right, Wrong, Good, Bad, All 9, POC, POD, Shorts, Boys and Beyonds.

Once again . . . take a deep breath . . . .
• What if you are not wrong?
• What if you've never been wrong?
• What if nothing you have ever said or ever done, has ever been wrong?

Everything that brings up, will you destroy and un-create it all?
Right, Wrong, Good, Bad, POC, POD, All 9, Shorts, Boys, and Beyonds.

SECRET . . . If you have no wrongness of you, you'll also never have the need or necessity of being right.

SECRET . . . If you believe that you're wrong, you see the world through "wrongness goggles." Have you ever commented on how beautiful someone was and they didn't receive it? That's because they believe they are wrong and their body is ugly. They are wearing "wrongness goggles." They experience their life, how they hear, feel, see, and touch, everything through those goggles. They won't allow themselves to receive money, a nurturing relationship or a beautiful body, because they are wrong. Does that wrongness make you feel lighter or heavier? Heavier, huh? That's because it's not true.

Everything that you think is so wrong about you, will you destroy and un-create all that?
Right, Wrong, Good, Bad, POC, POD, All 9, Shorts, Boys, and Beyonds.

Were you made wrong for just being? Did you ever get in trouble as a kid for laughing, or being joyful? If so, you were made wrong for being you.

Everything that brings up, will you destroy and un-create it all?
Right, Wrong, Good, Bad, POC, POD, All 9, Shorts, Boys, and Beyonds.

What if everything you think is wrong about you is really just a greatness about you you're not willing to receive?

Everything you have done to buy that wrongness, and not be, know, perceive, and receive the greatness you be, will you destroy and un-create it all?
Right, Wrong, Good, Bad, All 9, POC, POD, Shorts, Boys and Beyonds.

List some so-called "what you've decided is wrong with you" ideas you have of you from your point of view . . . .

• Can you see the greatness in you that you thought was a wrongness?

What you've decided is wrong with you (from your point of view) example:
I judge that I am overweight.
Everything that brings up, will you destroy and un-create it all?
Right, Wrong, Good, Bad, All 9, POC, POD, Shorts, Boys and Beyonds.

• What is the greatness you are unwilling to perceive about you? What talents, abilities and capacities do I have that I'm not acknowledging?

• Do you have a capacity for taking judgment out of other people's Universes? When you don't acknowledge your talents, abilities and capacities, your body tries to show you the greatness you're really doing and being.

What "you've decided is wrong with you" example: I have low self-esteem.
Everything that brings up, will you destroy and un-create it all?
Right, Wrong, Good, Bad, All 9, POC, POD, Shorts, Boys and Beyonds.

What is the greatness you are unwilling to perceive about you? Do you have a talent, ability, and capacity to pick up on other people's judgments? Good News, you're aware. Also, how much do you care? Have you ever made yourself inferior, so that other people didn't feel bad? That is actually an indication of how much you truly care. And, if you don't show up as the greatness you truly be, do they have the chance to perceive another possibility?

What you've decided is wrong with you:
Everything that brings up, will you destroy and un-create it all?
Right, Wrong, Good, Bad, All 9, POC, POD, Shorts, Boys and Beyonds.

• What is the greatness?

What you've decided is wrong with you:
Everything that brings up, will you destroy and un-create it all?
Right, Wrong, Good, Bad, All 9, POC, POD, Shorts, Boys and Beyonds.

• What is the greatness?

What you've decided is wrong with you:
Everything that brings up, will you destroy and un-create it all?
Right, Wrong, Good, Bad, All 9, POC, POD, Shorts, Boys and Beyonds.

• What is the greatness?

What you've decided is wrong with you:
Everything that brings up, will you destroy and un-create it all?
Right, Wrong, Good, Bad, All 9, POC, POD, Shorts, Boys and Beyonds.

• What is the greatness?

By you showing up as the greatness of you, you give everyone around you the opportunity to choose a greater possibility. What if you were the only chance that someone was going to have this lifetime to have a different choice? Would you be willing to choose it and show up as the greatness of you?

Everything you've done to not show up as the greatness of you, will you destroy and un-create all that?
Right, Wrong, Good, Bad, All 9, POC, POD, Shorts, Boys and Beyonds.

How many of you feel like, if you just got everything "perfect" then everything in your life would work? You wouldn't feel so wrong and other people wouldn't see you as wrong. Except perfection is a series of judgments that you're trying to fit into, and if you're trying to be perfect, how much do you have to judge you? Every moment. That's the trap of perfection. It's this unattainable goal that keeps you in a constant state of judgment of you.

Everything that brings up, will you destroy and un-create it all?
Right, Wrong, Good, Bad, POC, POD, All 9, Shorts, Boys, and Beyonds.

How many of you are trying to be perfect as if that was a way to avoid abuse? If I'm perfect, they'll love me. If I'm perfect, they won't leave me. If I'm perfect, they'll like me. If I'm perfect, they'll stop judging me.

Everything that brings up, will you destroy and un-create it all?
Right, Wrong, Good, Bad, POC, POD, All 9, Shorts, Boys, and Beyonds.

Here's a tool to get out of the paralysis of perfection and judgment until you don't judge you or anyone around you.

Just say, "You know what, I'm not going to judge myself here, and I don't have to be perfect", about everything.

How much judgment did you receive from your parents? Has anyone ever told you, "I'm the only one who loves you enough to tell you this, that skirt looks ugly on you." Is that love? Or, is that judgment and abuse.

Everywhere you have misidentified and misapplied love as judgment and judgment as love will you destroy and un-create all that?
Right, Wrong, Good, Bad, All 9, POC, POD, Shorts, Boys and Beyonds.

The incredible thing about that is, there is a level of judgment that is comfortable for you and makes you feel like, you are loving you, based on the level of judgment your parents perpetrated on you.

Everything that brings up, will you destroy and un-create it all?
Right, Wrong, Good, Bad, POC, POD, All 9, Shorts, Boys, and Beyonds.

How many of you were taught that in order to make yourself a better person (implying the pretence that you are wrong and bad) you must judge you.

Everything that brings up, will you destroy and un-create it all?
Right, Wrong, Good, Bad, POC, POD, All 9, Shorts, Boys, and Beyonds.

One of the amazing infinite beings in a session, once told me that she believed she was wrong for her body. She felt it was too big. When I asked her, what greatness that might be that she was unwilling to perceive. She couldn't see how it could be great in any way, until I asked her a few questions to unlock the energy. It turned out that she had the ability to "take on" energies, pain, suffering, and judgment from everyone around her. She believed this was the best way to change the world. I asked her to acknowledge how cool of a gift she was willing to be for others, and ran some clearing statements and the energy shifted. Suddenly, she could receive the talents, abilities and capacities she had been being, and was able to allow a change to occur for her.

If you were being totally conscious of all of your talents, abilities and capacities, would they ever create unconscious effects in your body or life? No, right? The target, here is to have you being, knowing, perceiving, and receiving the infinite Superhero you truly be.

What if you only had infinite space, caring and gratitude for you?

Another person actually felt like she was wrong for existing and being. I asked her if she could allow herself to be wrong in people's eyes who live from a place of judgment and conclusion, and have no point of view about them judging her. She had been receiving their judgments as painful and was going to the wrongness of her. This is where there was a lie attached with a truth. It is a truth that she is a beautiful, infinite being. It is a lie, that she is wrong for that. If you have no point of view, you can observe someone not receive you, judging you, judging themselves for it, and just remain that infinite space of generative energy, caring and gratitude.

Imagine being so full of life, so full of energy, so full of infinite space, and aware of all the infinite possibilities, and then running into a bunch of beings that operate from such a limited perspective that they cannot receive all that you be. They attempt to confine and limit you, so they can feel comfortable. They create judgments in order to not receive you. Any and every time this occurs, you naturally took on their points of view about the wrongness of you, instead of perceiving that their limitations would simply not allow for them to receive you . . . because if they received the infinite being you truly be . . . they would also receive themselves. You showed up being all this energy, space and consciousness. You had no judgments of you or anyone. You were being the oneness and consciousness of all things, and accepting and loving them totally. They refused to receive you. Do you think that might create a bit of confusion in your Universe?

Did they try to make you feel wrong about what you were being, to make them feel "okay" about them not receiving themselves. You most likely just wanted to feel connected to them, so you thought, "okay, I must adopt some of this wrongness." I am wrong. I won't do that, or be that again. Except, it happened enough times, that now you just think "the truth is, I'm wrong." However, if you have no point of view whether others can receive you or not, and how and why they judge you, then you will be free. These are the keys to the kingdom, unlocking the doorways to the secrets of the Universe, and you being you, all the time.

This is an excerpt from someone who took the "21 Secrets of the Universe" teleclass.

"My whole life, the people around me judged me and thought I was wrong. Even as a child. I have always been a free spirit, with joy, happiness and so much love and energy in my heart. My life has felt like crashing waves into rocks often, when I engage with others. I would show up, so happy and vibrant, only to leave feeling horrible about myself, like I just didn't fit in and there was something wrong with me. I was wrong for laughing too loud, being a little late, loving everyone, following my heart, being bored in school, not understanding this reality and even dreaming. Not only was I judged, but sometimes punished. I really believed that no matter what, I would just mess things up and do something wrong, so much so that I went the other way. I never liked being judged as wrong, so I kind of rebelled. And did it more, other times I would just completely contract and want to disappear. I bent over backwards to make others feel comfortable. If they were sad, I would try to find a way to meet them there. But, it never lasted for long, because my heart just wanted to be free. I wanted to play, to love, to dance, to create, to be free, to experience every drop of life. It felt like I didn't get the guidebook of rules when I was born. So many times I have asked just about everyone . . . "What is wrong with me?" Thinking if I could just locate the problem and then fix it. After coming across Access Consciousness™ and "21 Secrets of the Universe" I can truly perceive all the greatness about me, that I used to think was wrong. Now I can have allowance for what people choose, and not really turn it into anything to do with me. Sometimes I laugh, thinking about lifetimes where people probably killed me, just for me being me. Wow! It's not really about them though. It's about me choosing for

me, and loving, and caring for myself. And by the way, sometimes it's okay to invite new friends into your life. Ones that don't judge, control, confine, conclude, and limit you. And even if they, do, just have no point of view. I feel like the free spirit I have always been, and never allowed myself to experience. I have received a gift of more freedom through 21 Secrets of the Universe and I am very grateful."

Everything that is great and amazing about you, that you have turned into a wrongness of you instead of the greatness of you, will you destroy and un-create all of that now?
Right, Wrong, Good, Bad, All 9, POC, POD, Shorts, Boys and Beyonds.

Are you willing to be a generative energy, space and consciousness and sexualness that other people aren't willing to receive?
Everywhere you haven't been willing to be that, would you destroy and un-create it all?
Right, Wrong, Good, Bad, All 9, POC, POD, Shorts, Boys and Beyonds.

Another client shared that she felt like she scared men and was wrong for doing that. She had been unwilling to perceive that she wasn't wrong because they were choosing to shut off their receiving from her and run away. Like being a total "Being of Sexual Magnitude" is a bad thing! Yeah, right! It's awesome, a greatness, a complete generative energy of creation and contribution to living! After we worked with her clearing some of the energy and points of view around this, she is now able to turn up the heat whenever she chooses and also choose more men that can actually receive her and not go to the wrongness of her.

• When we can choose to be, know, perceive and receive our greatness, can we also then choose people in our lives that can also receive us more?

• What if the purpose of life is to just have fun?

Everywhere you are not willing to get the joke of the insane asylum most people are committed to on this planet, will you destroy and un-create all of that in it's entirety?
Right, Wrong, Good, Bad, All 9, POC, POD, Shorts, Boys and Beyonds.

• What if nothing was as important to you as you, and nothing was important enough to send yourself into judgment?

Everything that you think is important enough to you, to send you into judgment of you, like you said something that was wrong, did something, lost money, didn't follow your awareness, was "mean", every situation you feel like you must go into judgment of you, will you destroy and un-create all that?
Right, Wrong, Good, Bad, All 9, POC, POD, Shorts, Boys and Beyonds.

What if nothing was great enough to take you away from you? What if nothing was that important to you? Everything that doesn't allow that to show up, will you destroy and un-create it all?
Right, Wrong, Good, Bad, All 9, POC, POD, Shorts, Boys and Beyonds.

Do you know how many people walk around and make themselves wrong all the time? What is interesting about that is, "wrongness" is a choice they are making. You can acknowledge you as a being and know that all judgment is a lie, or you can shoot yourself down and kill you with the judgment of you. This is literally a key to the doorway out of this reality. It's one of the keys to your phenomenal life because you are never going to go into judgment of you again. Which opens your life up to the infinite possibilities.

• What if judgment wasn't mandatory?

• What if you lost your capacity to judge?

• What do you choose for you?

• Has the gift you be been received?

• Did you do everything you could to make those that didn't receive you right, so at least they didn't feel wrong?

What if you have to care for you, before you can care for anyone else? What if you cared so much for you that you became an inspiration for everyone else to find out how to care for themselves? What if you never sold yourself out for anyone else, ever? What if you cared so much for you, you never made them right, or yourself wrong in order to make them feel better?
Everything that doesn't allow for that will you destroy and un-create?
Right, Wrong, Good, Bad, All 9, POC, POD, Shorts, Boys and Beyonds.

The greatness is, you have been trying to do everything you could to make everyone else around you not go into judgment of themselves. Do you see how much caring there is in that?
You care so much, you would actually diminish you in order to not make them feel bad.

DID YOU KNOW YOU CAME HERE TO

BE THE CHANGE THAT CHANGES

THE WORLD?

Just by BEING you . . . .

Let's talk about your exercise for today.

Imagine your eyes are totally new and different eyes, the eyes of an alien of infinite space and gratitude. You view everything, including your body, with this generous gift of expanded love. This will allow you to undo all the areas where you think you are wrong, because you are the difference that changes the world.

Play with it, look at a tree for the first time . . . a caterpillar, your belly button, the pupils in your eyes, those cute adorable toes, a blade of grass . . . everything is new. You are in this awesome, amazing body, that is a sensory organ that is here to gift you with the orgasmic receiving of living with all the sounds, scents, tastes, perceptions, awareness, visions and experiences. This is a delightfully new adventure, for you, as a little alien, here now to make friends with your body and embrace all the molecules around you. You get to ask your body like you would a friend, what would you like to eat, to do, to be, where to go, who would you like to play with. You don't need to worry about anything, because your body will let you know everything. Just ask, and then listen.

Say "Hello" to your new best friend, your body. Feel your skin, those great hands, soft hair, lips, ears, beautiful thighs, bottom of the feet, fingernails. Put your hands on your face and say, "Thank you body, I am so grateful for you."

Now, also say "Hello" to this beautiful being called planet Earth and everything on it. Feel the connection your body has to the earth and the energy it is providing for your sweet body.

You can feel that you are the generative energy, space and consciousness that the Earth requires and is infinitely grateful for. Since, this is your first day here as this little, (BIG spaciousness) alien, everything is a question for you. And you have no judgments, conclusions or limitations, because you haven't been here long enough to even try and do that.

I know it might be strange to try and describe your first day in your body and on this planet, because it's all so new, but, go ahead and try to write about all your new friends, the body, the planet, and all of the molecules you are now interacting with as well as the amazing HUGE space and contribution you be!

You, are brand new here, now . . . .

As this alien you are infinite bliss, joy, and gratitude for every molecule. You know that the being you be and your infinite caring changes and transforms every being into knowing and receiving the infinite beings they truly be. You are in total knowing and celebration of the gift you are, to you, the planet and the world. Not everyone is willing to receive it, but that's okay, you are being it for you. If they receive it or not, that is their choice.

Everything you see is interesting, and fun. A whole new adventure, and you are the gift to every molecule there is.

Day 8 ❧ Secret of the Universe Daily Exercise

Imagine your eyes are totally new and different eyes, the eyes of an alien of infinite space and gratitude. You view everything, including your body, with this generous gift of expanded love. This will allow you to undo all the areas where you think you are wrong, because you are the difference that changes the world. Observe and experience your body, the planet, and this world with a new set of eyes. Then journal the unveiling of your magical adventurous day in the space below.

• What was your first day on planet Earth and in this fabulous body like?

• What did your body want?

• Where did you go?

• What did you see, hear, smell, feel?

• Who did you find out you really are?

Stop . . . See you tomorrow!

Day 10

Choosing your life in 10 second increments

DAILY EXERCISE:
Ask this question all day long, "If I had 10 seconds to live the rest of my life, what would I choose? Okay, that 10 seconds is up. If I had 10 seconds to live the rest of my life what would I choose?"

What if you began choosing your life in 10 second increments?

If you begin to choose your life in 10 second increments, you will begin creating your life from choice, instead of the "no choice Universe" most of the world functions within.

How do we create "a no-choice Universe?" Every judgment and conclusion creates the future of what you will allow yourself to choose. Anytime you find yourself automatically going into any energy based on an energy that is around you, that is a "no-choice Universe." Every reaction you go to from here on out is a indicator that you have a "no-choice Universe" and are reacting based on something that has occurred in your past.

Most people say, "Of course, I'm allowing myself to choose my life." My question is, "Is your life everything that you would like it to be right now?" If the answer is "no," then, are you actually choosing your life? Or, have you chosen your life? You have past conclusions and judgments "a no-choice Universe," that is keeping you from choosing everything you would truly like your life to be. Choice is your trump card. Choice is your potency. Choice will allow you to have the life you truly desire. If you would like to begin really choosing your life, we're going to need to practice.
Here's how this secret of the Universe exercise goes . . . .

If you had 10 seconds to live the rest of your life . . . what would you choose?

Okay, that 10 seconds is up, now what do you choose?
Okay, that 10 seconds is up, now what do you choose?
Okay, that 10 seconds is up, now what do you choose?
Okay, that 10 seconds is up, now what do you choose?

This will show you how much you don't choose for you and begin to allow you the freedom to begin a life and living where you choose for you every 10 seconds. How does it get any better than that?

The first step to choosing your life is getting out of judgment, conclusion, and perfection. The next step is CHOOSING in 10 second increments.

This will give you the capacity to receive all kinds of beautiful things and choose a phenomenal life from here on out.

Ready . . . you have infinite choice . . . .
"If I had 10 seconds to receive the rest of my life what would I choose?"

Okay, that 10 seconds is up . . . .
"If I had 10 seconds to receive the rest of my life what would I choose?"

Okay, that 10 seconds is up . . . .
"If I had 10 seconds to receive the rest of my life what would I choose?"

When you choose in 10 second increments, you are always in choice and always present to receive. Any choice that lasts for more than 10 seconds is actually a conclusion.

When you are choosing for you, do you get more of you or less?
What if everything is just a choice for that 10 seconds? Your phenomenal life, your car, your consciousness, your words, your body, your money, your love life, and all of your points of view. You have complete choice in everyway, in everyday, to choose for you. The more you find yourself choosing for you, the more you will begin to have your life be everything you choose it to be.

I had a session with a healer, practitioner, and she was having a difficult time "choosing for her." She always chose for how others needed her instead of choosing for her. She hesitated when it came to choosing for her because she judged that choosing for her was bad. She thought that if she chose for herself, others would judge her to be selfish and self-centered . . . Let me ask you this, if you won't allow yourself to choose for you, as an honoring of you, is anyone going to do it for you? What if choosing for you didn't mean that you have to choose against others?

Everything that doesn't allow you to choose for you, will you destroy and un-create all that?
Right, Wrong, Good, Bad, POC, POD, All 9, Shorts, Boys and Beyonds™.

Even if choosing in 10 second increments feels like it's hard to remember, or a little like having ADD or ADHD, it is one of the keys to the kingdom to having everything you desire out of life.

If you had 10 seconds to choose the rest of your life, would you judge you? Would you judge your husband, wife, or partner? Would you hold onto past grudges and suppressed anger?

Or, would you take that last 10 seconds to express your gratitude for them. Would all of that energy that you use to separate you from the ones you love most, fall away as if it doesn't exist? You know why it wouldn't exist? Because it's a lie.

Okay. Right now, let's do an exercise called "making it infinite." This is an incredible way to find out if something is a truth or a lie. Close your eyes. Think about someone with whom you're upset. Pull all that energy up in your awareness. Now, begin expanding it out until it's as big as the Universe. Did it get more substantial or disappear? It disappeared, huh? That's because it's a lie.

Now close your eyes and think about someone that makes your heart smile, someone you're totally grateful for. It could be a pet, a lover, or a friend. Expand that out as big as the Universe. Did it get more substantial or disappear? It got more substantial, huh? That's because it's true.

NOTE: If the upset didn't disappear, run, "Everything I'm unwilling to let go of here, everywhere I'm invested in me being "right" and then being "wrong," I will now destroy and un-create all that."
Right, Wrong, Good, Bad, POC, POD, All 9, Shorts, Boys and Beyonds™.

• Choice Creates Presence

Let's do this. Right now call or get in the presence of someone you love and say to yourself, "If I had 10 seconds to live the rest of my life, what would I choose to say to this person? And say it. What energy would I choose to receive? Receive it. If you're in an intimate relationship ask them, "Can I kiss you?" and in your head say, "If I had 10 seconds to choose the rest of my life, how much would I receive. I'm choosing to kiss this person."

Wasn't that fun? How much did you receive? How present were you? Doesn't that make you want to really choose your life in 10 second increments?

When you choose in every moment, you receive every moment. Isn't that so amazing? Choice actually creates presence. When you are present, you are actually receiving. If you could eliminate the judgment of you and others and begin choosing for you in every moment, imagine all of which you would be aware. Imagine what you could choose to receive. Imagine what contribution to the world you could be.

If you ever feel like you are choosing for other people and not you, ask, "If I was choosing this all for me, what energy would I be?"

Day 10 ❧ Secret of the Universe Daily Exercise

STEP 1: Ask this question all day, "If I had 10 seconds to live the rest of my life, what would I choose?"

STEP 2: Then say, "Okay, that 10 seconds is up. If I had 10 seconds to live the rest of my life, what would I choose?"

STEP 3: Allow yourself to be a little crazy today. Choose to walk, then run, then eat food, then sing, then chocolate ice cream, or vanilla, or strawberry, or . . . etcetera. Allow yourself to drive everyone nuts. Just for today, it's Okay. You're practicing your new life of choice!

Choose in Every Moment,

Receive every Moment . . . .

Stop . . . See you tomorrow!

Day II

Choosing your life in IO second increments and following the energy

DAILY EXERCISE:
Ask this question all day long, "If I had 10 seconds to live the rest of my life, what would I choose?" Allow that question to open up a doorway to perceiving what that choice will create and choose based on following the energy.

Now that you've chosen in 10 second increments, we are going to add another awareness.

Choosing in 10 second increments and Perceiving and Following the Energy

PERCEIVING ENERGY
Some people believe that they can't perceive energy. Have you ever hugged someone and your body just melted? Have you also hugged someone and felt like you were hugging a brick wall? If so, you can perceive energy. If you feel like you can't perceive energy now, don't worry. As this information continues to expand your Universe you are going to have more awareness and capacity to perceive energy.

If you have any conclusion or judgment about the energy you're perceiving, you are wearing goggles that cut off your awareness. You can't totally perceive energy unless you have no judgment or conclusion about what you're perceiving. You are wearing filters that you are perceiving your awareness through. Say you are thinking about having sex with somebody and wondering whether your body would like to have sex with them, too. In order to have a clear awareness go to the bathroom and create a bubble of energy around you. **THEN:**

Destroy and un-create all my decisions, judgments, conclusions, computations, projections, rejections, and expectations about me having sex with them and everything I'm picking up about them wanting to have sex with me.
Right, Wrong, Good, Bad, POC, POD, All 9, Shorts, Boys and Beyonds™.

Then muscle test your body to find out whether your body would like to have sex with them.

WHAT IF YOU CAN TRUST YOU?

Some people feel like they can't trust their awareness and the energy they are perceiving. What if you can trust your awareness? What if, what you can't trust is your judgments or conclusions? A few months ago I was planning a trip to Australia and my passport was screaming, "Pay attention to me!" I went to look for it and couldn't find it anywhere. I asked, "Passport, where are you?" and it showed me that it was at my friend's house. I called him and asked and he said, "Yes, I have your passport." I took a deep breath and concluded, "That is what the energy was around my passport." Was that a question or conclusion? A conclusion. The next question I could have asked was, "Was that the energy around my passport? Is there anything I else I need to be aware of here?" But, I didn't ask another question. I showed up at the airport all ready to fly to Australia and guess what? My passport expired three days prior to my travel. Can I not trust me? Or can I not trust my conclusion? I had the awareness about the passport and can trust me. What I can't trust is any conclusion or judgment.

When you are choosing in every moment, you are being in the moment. Anything that you choose will show up. Except, in this reality a "no-choice Universe" is constantly being presented. Anytime you create a judgment or conclusion, the elimination of choice occurs. If you are choosing in 10 second increments and reading or perceiving the energy and choosing what makes you feel lighter, you are free to choose for you and be in the moment. Have you ever chosen something, and then right at the moment to actually follow through with that choice, it feels contracted or heavy? But you still went ahead and did it anyway? That's what we call denying your knowing. Have you ever known you shouldn't get into a relationship and then talked yourself into it, and it turned out just the way you knew it was going to? The truth is, you always know. What would it be like to never deny your knowing ever again? Take a second and make that promise to you . . . .

"I will never deny my knowing ever again."

Everything that brings up, will you destroy and un-create it all?
Right, Wrong, Good, Bad, POC, POD, All 9, Shorts, Boys, and Beyonds.

One of the ways people really eliminate their choice is by judging whether their choices are "right" or "wrong."

When you judge your choices as "right" or "wrong" here is how you limit you:

1. If you judge your choices before you make them, you cut off your awareness of what the future of what that choice will create. If you judge that you are making the "right" choice, you can't be aware of anything that won't turn out "right" about the choice you just made. Just as if you judge your choice is "wrong" you won't allow yourself to receive anything that could be "right" or a gift about making that choice.

2. If you judge your choices, you create "no-choice Universe" in the future. If you judged that one of your choices is "right," you'll tend to make the same choice in the future, even if it's twenty years later, and you're a new person, living in a new Universe. If you judge your choice as "wrong," you'll never see what could be "right" about the choice you made. Also, you'll never allow yourself to make the same choice, even if it could actually work for you in the future.

If you judge your choice before you choose, here's how you limit you. How many of you look at all the pros (rights) and cons (wrongs) before you'll allow yourself to choose? This particular matrix is a killer because everyone wants to make the "right" choice. If you decide that one of your choices is right, you'll never allow yourself to choose again. I had one private session with a client who was in a bad marriage. I asked her, "When did you know that you shouldn't have gotten married?" Her answer was, "six months before the wedding." I asked, "How long have you been unhappy in your marriage?" She said "sixteen years." Wow, since she had created the judgment that she was doing the "right" thing, and making the "right" choice, she followed through for sixteen years in a marriage that didn't work for her. She couldn't make a different choice because she didn't want to be "wrong." What if no choice was "right" or "wrong?" What if all choice was just choice?

Every choice you've ever made that you have judged as "right" or "wrong" instead of just "a choice," will you destroy and un-create all that?
Right, Wrong, Good, Bad, POC, POD, All 9, Shorts, Boys and Beyonds™.

CHOICE CREATES AWARENESS
Choosing in 10 second increments and following the energy, allows you to be aware of what your choice will create, because choice creates awareness. Right now, think about the one thing you think is impossible that would expand your business or life exponentially . . . .

What would expand my life exponentially?
For me, I choose to get on a talk show and invite millions of people to consciousness.

When I choose that in this moment, and say "yes," energy is surging through my body. Choosing something creates an awareness of "the energy" of what the future of that choice will create. Also, in choosing it, I know it's coming, as long as I don't create any conflicting points of view. Like, "That would scare me, I could never do that, I would be too embarrassed . . . etcetera," you get the picture. Also, everything that is required to change in my Universe to allow that to show up will now come into my life and all I have to do is follow the energy. What people don't know is choice is your "Trump Card." If you choose it, whatever you're choosing will show up.

What could you choose right now that would expand your life exponentially?

I choose _____

_____

_____

How do you feel? Is your heart racing a bit? Is there more excitement? That is an awareness about the exciting future that choice will create.

I choose _____

_____

_____

What are you energetically perceiving?

_____

_____

I choose _____

_____

_____

What are you energetically perceiving?

_____

_____

I choose _____

_____

_____

What are you energetically perceiving?

_____

_____

I choose _____

_____

_____

What are you energetically perceiving?

_____

_____

_____

I choose _____

_____

_____

WELCOME TO CHOOSING YOUR EXCITING, FUN, JOYFUL LIFE!

For how many of you did it "feel" like you were "scared" or had "fear?" Does "fear" make you feel lighter or heavier? Heavier, huh? What if "fear" was basically a lie that you use to eliminate choice and distracts you from being present? Neurologically there is no difference between fear and excitement. This reality has taught us that excitement is "fear" so that we'll stop ourselves. Some people think that "fear" keeps them safe. Let me ask you this, "What would be more beneficial; fear or awareness?" Awareness, huh? Eliminate the word "fear" from your dictionary and call it excitement so that you never stop you from your exciting life.

All the programs of fear that you have implanted into your reality, will you destroy and un-create all that?
Right, Wrong, Good, Bad, POC, POD, All 9, Shorts, Boys and Beyonds™.

All the places that you have stopped you based on that fear, will you unlock all that energy, and open the floodgates of receiving an exciting life? Everything that is will you destroy and un-create it all?
Right, Wrong, Good, Bad, POC, POD, All 9, Shorts, Boys and Beyonds™.

Did you know that any choice that lasts for more than 10 seconds is a conclusion?

To receive all the magic of the Universe, if you perceive the energy, and choose, and be present in the moment, you can receive and create anything. For instance, if you ask for a new car, a new car is on the way. The Universe is delivering the car, but wait, if you have all these judgments and conclusions in the way, will you be able to follow the energy? If you aren't choosing, being present in the moment, or creating judgments and conclusions about the car you are limiting the infinite ways the Universe is attempting to gift to you.

This key to the kingdom will unlock so much receiving, your life might become a tsunami of receiving the magic and potency you truly be.

The Universe will knock and knock and knock at your door to deliver the amazing phenomenal life for which you've asked. Just a little secret: you must choose it. Choose to have it. Choose in 10 second increments. Choose to follow the energy. Choose it when it shows up.

Have you ever known anyone who so badly desires to have an intimate relationship in their life, yet every single person who shows up to fulfill that desire, they judge and conclude about how they aren't what they want? Interesting, huh?

I had a client once who went so far down the path of conclusion . . . that every time the Universe attempted to deliver a different possibility she refused it. She owned several properties and the market was crashing. She had concluded that the only way she could get out from underneath her properties was to declare bankruptcy. A family member offered to buy one of her properties. Did she receive it? Or refuse it? She refused it. Then one of her tenants called to ask if she could create a lease with the option to buy. Did she receive it? Or refuse it? She refused it. The Universe was knocking on the door, offering other possibilities, but she had already concluded and therefore couldn't receive any other possibilities. She had decided and concluded that was the only way. So guess what, it was.

The more solidified a person is in their conclusions, the less they will be able to be aware of anything else. Every time you go into judgment, anything that doesn't match that judgment can't even come into your awareness. Which creates a "no-choice Universe."

What if you choose for you, no matter what it takes, no matter what occurs, no matter who leaves your life, no matter what happens?

CHOICE CREATES AWARENESS AND PRESENCE

What if being the space of no judgment for you and everyone around you brought you more money than you can even imagine? Everyone wants to not judge themselves. So when you can be that space of no judgment, they'll want what you have, and they'll want to pay you for it.

There was one client who felt like she couldn't show up as the joyful, wonderful, beautiful infinite being she truly is in public. Every time she chose to show up as her she was riddled with judgments of herself, people would not like her or want to get close to her, she would shut herself down, contract and run away. During the exercise of choosing in 10 second increments she went to her daughter's class party and joyfully danced and sang and she chose to not judge herself every 10 seconds. For the first time she could be herself in public, and said the other moms actually came up to her and hugged her and wanted to be friends. She was gloriously excited and liberated by choosing to not judge her in 10 second increments!

I asked her, "When you were choosing to not judge you in 10 second increments, were you actually undoing everyone else's judgments of themselves around you?" She said, "What? You mean those were never my judgments of myself? You mean I was picking up on other people judging me and thought I was judging me?" I said, "Yes, and they were judging you in order to not receive that playful, joyful, energy you were being. Every 10 seconds that you chose not to judge you, you actually unraveled their judgments of themselves."

We know that people will judge us if we are being an energy that they are not willing to be in order to keep their judgments of themselves and their reality in place. If you don't judge you, others will have less ability to judge you and themselves. For one, if people judge you and you don't go into judgments of you or them, they'll stop judging you because it's not working to shut you down. Secondly, in the space of no judgment it takes too much energy to hold any judgments in place. Have you ever been in the presence of the Dali Lama? Did you notice that after awhile, you have no judgments or thoughts in your head? Would you be willing to be the space of no judgments for you and others and change the world just by being?

Day II ∽ Secret of the Universe Daily Exercise

Choosing in 10 second increments and perceiving and following the energy. "If I had 10 seconds to live the rest of my life, what would I choose?"

STEP 1: Keep choosing your life in 10 second increments, and perceive and follow the energy.

STEP 2: Choose what makes you feel lighter.

STEP 3: Destroy and un-create all your decisions, judgments, computations and conclusions you have around the choice.

STEP 4: See if the choice still makes you feel lighter, and choose it.
(Remember the difference between judgment and awareness: awareness will always make you feel lighter, judgment always has a polarity attached.)

Stop . . . See you tomorrow!

Day 12

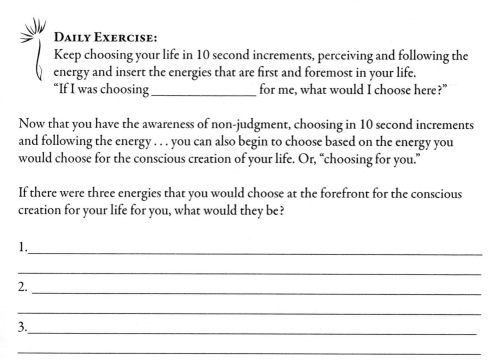

Choosing in 10 second increments what energies you choose for your life

DAILY EXERCISE:
Keep choosing your life in 10 second increments, perceiving and following the energy and insert the energies that are first and foremost in your life.
"If I was choosing _____ for me, what would I choose here?"

Now that you have the awareness of non-judgment, choosing in 10 second increments and following the energy . . . you can also begin to choose based on the energy you would choose for the conscious creation of your life. Or, "choosing for you."

If there were three energies that you would choose at the forefront for the conscious creation for your life for you, what would they be?

1._____
_____

2. _____
_____

3._____
_____

Some of the energies I have at the forefront of my reality are:

1. No judgment and being the space of caring for me and everyone.

2. Fun, joy, playfulness and ease.

3. Getting in front of as many people as possible as quickly as possible to facilitate as much consciousness as possible and change the world.

Most people have the point of view that they don't know how to choose, or what they would choose for themselves.

Let me ask you this, "What percentage of your life have you chosen for you?" _____%

For most people it's around 5%, and they have the point of view that they are "bad" at choosing for themselves. So if you've only been really choosing 5% of your life for you, are you actually "bad" at choosing for you, or are you terrible at choosing based on other people's points of view? What if it is actually really easy for you to choose for you?

How much of your choices have been based on everybody else's point of view? Including the point of view that you don't even know how or what to choose for you? Everything that brings up, will you destroy and un-create it all? Right, Wrong, Good, Bad, POC, POD, All 9, Shorts, Boys and Beyonds.

If you don't know what you desire, and don't allow yourself to choose it, does it make sense that it hasn't really shown up yet? If joy and fun are at the foremost of my reality, I will choose based on that. I will choose to have more money in my life because it provides more fun, joy, and ease. I will arrive early at the airport because I choose fun, joy and ease. I will create a fun, joyful, and ease-filled experience because that is what I choose. I also choose to change the world. So anywhere I go I am choosing to be the space of no judgment that will unravel the limitations around me. I will show up anywhere and anytime because that is one of the energies that is at the forefront of my reality. When I am choosing what is at the forefront of my reality I know I am the captain of my own ship and I am choosing for me.

A lot of people put "things" before energy. They think, "If I had the money, then I could be joyful." The choice to choose joy whether you have the money or not comes before the money showing up. What if money follows joy? What if you were willing to receive lots of money just because it was joyful or fun for you, not the source of your joy, but an addition to the intensity and fullness of joy you are already choosing? A lot of people think the joy of money is spending money. If you like spending money more than you like having it, you actually hate money.

Everything that brings up for you, will you destroy and un-create it all? Right, Wrong, Good, Bad, POC, POD, All 9, Shorts, Boys and Beyonds.

Sometimes in the beginning of people choosing for themselves I observe them choosing against others, as if that was "choosing for them." Choosing for you doesn't necessitate choosing against others. In fact, when you are really choosing for you, you will include others in your choices and not do what is going to create an upset. You care about every being, and also don't want to have their unhappiness haunting your awareness, because you're psychic and will receive the information. What it will feel like is you think you're thinking contractively about them. Remember, "Am I thinking about them, or are they thinking about me?" When you are truly choosing for you, you will also allow yourself to have the awareness of what your choices will bring for you and everyone. Here is where it gets sticky for some people.

My friend was telling me about some experience she created in her life, where she believed she was choosing for her. There was a certain amount of fall-out from the other people involved. She didn't go to the wrongness of her, luckily. But she didn't understand what had happened. She said, "Honestly, I was just choosing for me and in my world it all made sense, I didn't even think that anyone would be mad at me, and I chose what I wanted." I asked her if she would be willing to have the awareness of what the future of her choices would be for her and everyone. If she had been willing to look at where the other people involved were going to be affected by her choices, choosing for her might have looked different.

Sometimes choosing for you is actually choosing something that may feel heavy in the moment, but lighter when you include the future in your awareness. A client of mine's sister was getting married and when she thought of being in Los Angeles with her sister and all of her friends the energy wasn't light. Yet, she was the maid of honor. I asked her to also be aware of what the future of not going would create. Her sister would have been devastated and their relationship would have suffered. When she looked at the whole picture, she knew what to choose.

When I am going to an event or something, I ask my clothes, "Which one of you wants to be worn?" I ask for the awareness. Not because I am being controlled by the judgments of other people, but because I desire to create connection, not separation. Of course, I can wear the craziest, sexiest thing I own, and receive any judgments that might come my way, but if I have the awareness that to wear something else would be more expansive for the people with whom I interact, then I will. You can still choose to do or be something even if you have the awareness that it will create separation or a mess to clean up, or you can choose what would work for everyone as well. It's just a choice.

Living your life from awareness will help to create a beautiful bridge to your dreams unfolding for you. You know that you are never wrong for any choices you make, and you also know the future your choices will create. You can truly "choose for you" all the time. Gary Douglas always says that people don't want to look at the future because they think they won't like what they see, when actually it would allow the awareness for them to really choose and create the life they would truly like to have.

One of my clients said she didn't really allow herself to consciously look into the future of some of her choices because she felt like it took away some of the mystery, delight and surprise of all the possibilities. I could perceive her energy around this, she was like a little kid, that didn't want to know what was in the boxes wrapped under the Christmas tree until Christmas morning. She loved that excitement of not knowing, until things were unwrapped.

She also did this with the choices of relationship and money, really cute. We ran some clearings on her and unlocked the energy. Now she can see every experience as Christmas morning and a miracle, and also allow herself to check in on the future before choosing. Imagine if you could perceive the energy of the future of everything you think, do, say, be and choose. Does it feel like your life would be easier and more expansive? By choosing in 10 second increments this becomes your way of being. You know the future of every choice, and the future that will be created with everything you think, do, say, and be.

Everything that brings up for you, will you destroy and un-create it all?
Right, Wrong, Good, Bad, POC, POD, All 9, Shorts, Boys and Beyonds.

Day 12 ∾ Secret of the Universe Daily Exercise

What are the top 3 energies for the conscious creation of your life?

ENERGY #1_____

ENERGY #2_____

ENERGY #3_____

STEP 1: Keep choosing your life in 10 second increments and insert these energies.

Fill in the blanks: If I were choosing _____ for me here, what would I choose? Okay, I'll choose that.

For example, If <u>joy</u> is one of your energies and someone cuts you off in traffic then ask, "If I were choosing what is joyful for me here what would I choose?" Oh, to make him Yosemite Sam and laugh at how his face is bright red there is smoke coming out of his ears.

If <u>the space of caring</u> is one of your energies and someone is judging you ask, "If I was <u>the space of caring</u> here what would I choose?" I would choose to be the space of caring for me here no matter what they choose. And I would know that they are judging me because I am being an energy that they are not willing to be. I would not judge them back, and know they are probably even more mean and judgmental to themselves.

Sometimes choosing for you is not logical, linear, responsible or reasonable. If you get an e-mail from someone going on and on about how terrible of a person you are, and you think that's funny is that logical, or reasonable? No, but if <u>joy</u> is one of the foremost energies for the conscious creation of your life, then you are choosing for you.

Doesn't this tool give you a different awareness on what choosing for you actually means and "how" to choose for you? Enjoy today, the first day of you choosing FOR YOU.

NOTES: _____

_____

_____

_____

_____

_____

_____

_____

_____

Stop . . . See you tomorrow!

Day 13

Validation of Other People's Realities

DAILY EXERCISE:
Keep working (or playing) with, "If I was choosing _____ for me what would I choose here?" If resistance comes up, ask, "What creation of <u>this energy</u> am I using to validate everybody else's realities?"

How much of your life have you created in order to validate everyone else's realities? Where do you learn how to limit, judge and define you? From you? Or from the world around you? Validation of other people's realities is where you are making other people's limitations right or true.

How much of your life, your choice, and everything about you, is based on everyone else's points of view?
Everything that brings up would you destroy and un-create it all?
Right, Wrong, Good, Bad, POC, POD, All 9, Shorts, Boys and Beyonds™.

This secret is really fun because it's actually quite entertaining. In our own lives we have just begun to choose for us, and became aware of how little we actually have done that. The only way that any of us have learned limitation is from watching everyone else, and attempting to choose our lives based on their realities. It's like we have created ourselves as limited, too, otherwise we would totally undo through their realities. We've all been the space that unravels people's limitations as well. It's not always fun receiving other people's reactions and judgments when we don't validate their limitations.

Have you ever had a friend that only wanted to complain about their life? Isn't it strange how if you don't validate that for them, they don't really want to talk to you? What's even better, is you spent so much of your time attempting to "help" them or inspire them in new ways or be a good listener or friend, and that is not what they even wanted. What they actually desire is for you to validate how it's not their fault, they are a victim and the whole world is doing this to them.

What percentage of your life have you chosen for you? _____ %. So, about _____% of your life is being run by other people's points of view. This is where you are creating your life in order to validate other people's realities. What if the _____% of your life that you're choosing for you is the _____% of your life that is actually working for you? What if the _____% of your life that you're not choosing for you is the _____% of your life that is not working for you? What would it be like to choose 1000% of your life for you?

Everywhere you are choosing and creating your life to validate other people's realities, will you destroy and un-create all that?
Right, Wrong, Good, Bad, POC, POD, All 9, Shorts, Boys and Beyonds™.

The key to unlock this is using this clearing statement.

What creation of _____ am I using to validate other people's realities?

Everything that brings up, and everywhere you've created your life, your money flows, your body and your relationships based on everyone else, will you destroy and un-create all that?
Right, Wrong, Good, Bad, POC, POD, All 9, Shorts, Boys and Beyonds™.

Anytime something that you truly desire isn't showing up, you might want to look at all the points of view you have around it. Then ask, "Is this truly my point of view? Or someone else's?" Guess what? You may find out that they were not even yours in the first place. Have you ever watched the evening news? Can you imagine if you bought into all those view points as true? You probably wouldn't even want to leave your house again. Yet, look at how many people unconsciously listen to, align, agree, resist and react to all of those points of view that are locking that reality into place.

Everything that brings up, will you destroy and un-create it all?
Right, Wrong, Good, Bad, POC, POD, All 9, Shorts, Boys and Beyonds™.

I'm a singer/songwriter and for two years I had been asking and asking, "What would it take for a record deal to show up?" "What would it take for a record deal to show up?" "What would it take for a record deal to show up?" Finally I asked, what points of view do I have here that are not allowing this to come to fruition? I thought, "I didn't want to lose my anonymity. I didn't want to go on a tour bus for months with drunk people. If I had that much fame, success, and money I wouldn't know who my "real" friends were. I didn't want anyone to be able to "own me." Do any of those points of view have anything to do with how I would create a record deal? Would I choose alcoholic musicians or conscious ones? Would I lose my anonymity? Or would I be able to disappear anytime I chose? Would I really not know who my "real" friends were? Or would I always know? If I were owned by a record company that flew me all over the world, put me on stages, magazines, TV, etcetera. would it be "so bad" to be owned by that? No. I was creating the refusal of the record deal based on everyone else's reality. None of that had anything to do with how I would actually choose it. Finally I asked, "What creation of record deal am I using to validate everyone else's reality? I destroyed and un-created all those points of view and within twenty-four hours I was being offered a deal by Elton John's producer, Greg Penny! He came in a bar which I was playing and said, "I had a dream about you last night. It's time. Would you like to make a record together?" Literally twenty-four hours later!!! What if you are that powerful? What if you could let go of all of the points of view that are keeping you from having your dreams come true, and they actually would?

Every point of view you've taken based on everyone else's realities that is keeping you from having your dreams come true, will you destroy and un-create all that? Right, Wrong, Good, Bad, POC, POD, All 9, Shorts, Boys and Beyonds™.

List some things that would be a "dream come true" for you . . . .

DREAM:_____

_____

POINTS OF VIEW THAT AREN'T ALLOWING IT TO SHOW UP _____

_____

_____

_____

_____

_____

_____

DREAM:_____

_____

POINTS OF VIEW THAT AREN'T ALLOWING IT TO SHOW UP _____

_____

_____

_____

_____

_____

_____

_____

_____

DREAM:_____

_____

_____

POINTS OF VIEW THAT AREN'T ALLOWING IT TO SHOW UP _____

_____

_____

_____

_____

_____

_____

_____

Everything that makes these dreams instead of realities, will you destroy and un-create it all?
Right, Wrong, Good, Bad, POC, POD, All 9, Shorts, Boys and Beyonds™.

One of my beautiful clients described this secret as a light bulb moment. When I shared this tool with her, she said it felt a little like getting hit over the head. She was dizzy and so excited at the same time. She immediately was able to look at how she had been not allowing her dreams to come true by taking points of view that would stop them from occurring.

Would you be willing to allow your dreams to come true?
Everything that brings up, will you destroy and un-create it all?
Right, Wrong, Good, Bad, POC, POD, All 9, Shorts, Boys and Beyonds™.

Take a moment, to celebrate you right now. Because you are reading this, it does mean that you are choosing more for you. Stretch your arms out really big to say thank you to the Universe. Now wrap those arms around your body and say thank you to you!

If you ever feel like you have gone on autopilot during your day and are not choosing for you, just recognize it and ask, "If I had 10 seconds to live the rest of my life, what would I choose?" If you are actually willing to look at how many points of view you are using to create your life that don't even belong to you, you would laugh, and begin choosing for you. Have you ever had a big dream, like changing the world, or becoming a rock star, or a famous artist, or President? I love the movie Kung Fu Panda, because the panda always knew he wanted more for his life. Here he was a great big panda bear, working with his dad, as was this little goose, cooking noodles. He would dream of becoming this great kung fu master and everyone would just laugh at him. His dad would tell him that he, too, had once had dreams of a better and different life, but those didn't come true, and to just be happy and accept the life he was living.

How many of us have accepted those points of view and completely limited all the infinite possibilities of expansion beyond our wildest dreams from showing up? How many of us were taught by our parents to prepare for the disappointment of life?

If you are doing this you would then create your life as a disappointment in order to validate their realities.
Everything that brings up, will you destroy and un-create it all?
Right, Wrong, Good, Bad, POC, POD, All 9, Shorts, Boys and Beyonds™.

So everywhere that you have bought into and created a life of mediocrity based on everyone else's points of view, will you destroy and un-create it through all time, space, dimensions and realities?
Right, Wrong, Good, Bad, POC, POD, All 9, Shorts, Boys and Beyonds™.

Look at how many times we create and re-create all of these limited points of view from the past? Do these really even exist? Has anyone ever told you the point of view that history always repeats itself? Wonder why? You hold it in place with every judgment and conclusion about it. Is time real? Or is time a construct? A construct. Anytime you run a clearing statement and let go of limitation, it changes for you and everyone you bought and sold it to from any lifetime. So every time we run the clearing statement at least 350,000 other people get free. So does the past really exist? Or can the past change if you choose to change it? If you let go of your past in its entirety, would you have more possibility or less?

Everything that brings up, will you destroy and un-create it all?
Right, Wrong, Good, Bad, POC, POD, All 9, Shorts, Boys and Beyonds™.

If you choose to use this tool, "What creation of _____ am I using to validate other people's realities?" In every area of your life you would begin to know what you would actually choose for you. If something isn't working, you can just say to yourself "Okay, I must have created this based on somebody else's point of view. If I were having it all for me, what would it be like, feel like and what would I choose here?" Here is another secret: when you choose it, it makes everyone else's realities fall away. The only time you have ever stopped you is when you were doing something that didn't work for you. The next question is, "What would work for you?" and choose that.

Everything that brings up, will you destroy and un-create it all?
Right, Wrong, Good, Bad, POC, POD, All 9, Shorts, Boys and Beyonds™.

What if the exact percentage of choosing for other people's realities is the exact percentage of your life that isn't working for you right now? What if you are the element in your life that actually works? Everyone else's points of views and realities inserted into your reality is the element that is creating what isn't working for you?

Everything that brings up, will you destroy and un-create it all?
Right, Wrong, Good, Bad, POC, POD, All 9, Shorts, Boys and Beyonds™.

Just like in Kung Fu Panda, when he was to become the great dragon warrior and in the sacred scroll, he was to find the secret ingredient. Except when he opened it, all he saw was his own reflection. What if you're the one thing that does work about your life? What if the secret ingredient is you? Yet, how often do we search for more of us in everything else? Like, when I get the perfect guy or girl, then I'll have more of me. When my career takes off, then I will be ... When ... When ... When ... What if none of those things have ever been the source of you having more of you? What if you are the one you have been looking for? What if the only time anything in your life has ever given you more of you, was because you chose more of you?

Everything you are unwilling to be, know, perceive and receive about all of that, will you destroy and un-create it all?
Right, Wrong, Good, Bad, POC, POD, All 9, Shorts, Boys and Beyonds™.

What creation of <u>my current financial situation</u> am I using to validate everyone else's realities?
Everything that brings up, will you destroy and un-create it all?
Right, Wrong, Good, Bad, POC, POD, All 9, Shorts, Boys and Beyonds™.

What creation of _____ am I using to validate everyone else's realities?
Everything that brings up, will you destroy and un-create it all?
Right, Wrong, Good, Bad, POC, POD, All 9, Shorts, Boys and Beyonds™.

What creation of _____ am I using to
validate everyone else's realities?
Everything that brings up, will you destroy and un-create it all?
Right, Wrong, Good, Bad, POC, POD, All 9, Shorts, Boys and Beyonds™.

What creation of _____ am I using to
validate everyone else's realities?
Everything that brings up, will you destroy and un-create it all?
Right, Wrong, Good, Bad, POC, POD, All 9, Shorts, Boys and Beyonds™.

What creation of _____ am I using to
validate everyone else's realities?
Everything that brings up, will you destroy and un-create it all?
Right, Wrong, Good, Bad, POC, POD, All 9, Shorts, Boys and Beyonds™.

What creation of _____ am I using to
validate everyone else's realities?
Everything that brings up, will you destroy and un-create it all?
Right, Wrong, Good, Bad, POC, POD, All 9, Shorts, Boys and Beyonds™.

What creation of _____ am I using to
validate everyone else's realities?
Everything that brings up, will you destroy and un-create it all?
Right, Wrong, Good, Bad, POC, POD, All 9, Shorts, Boys and Beyonds™.

What creation of _____ am I using to
validate everyone else's realities?
Everything that brings up, will you destroy and un-create it all?
Right, Wrong, Good, Bad, POC, POD, All 9, Shorts, Boys and Beyonds™.

What creation of _____ am I using to
validate everyone else's realities?
Everything that brings up, will you destroy and un-create it all?
Right, Wrong, Good, Bad, POC, POD, All 9, Shorts, Boys and Beyonds™.

What creation of _____ am I using to
validate everyone else's realities?
Everything that brings up, will you destroy and un-create it all?
Right, Wrong, Good, Bad, POC, POD, All 9, Shorts, Boys and Beyonds™.

Day 13 ❧ Secret of the Universe Daily Exercise

STEP 1: If I were choosing _____ for me, what would I choose?

STEP 2: If resistance comes up, then ask, "What creation of <u>this energy</u> am I using to validate everybody else's realities?" The only time you'll ever feel resistance is when you are attempting to choose based on everyone else's points of view.

NOTES: _____

_____

_____

_____

_____

_____

_____

_____

_____

_____

_____

_____

_____

_____

_____

_____

Stop . . . See you tomorrow!

Day 14

ᘒ

The secret ingredient for your life is YOU!

DAILY EXERCISE:
Pull over, and get out of the Pinto®. Get out of the judgment and conclusion reality and realize you are the active ingredient that makes anything work. Begin running the clearing statement: "What secret agenda with _____ am I using to maintain and entrain _____? This will begin unlocking all of the limitations you've created in any lifetime that are running your life.

Have you ever thought . . . "If only I just have this money or success, or get this relationship, or if I can just lose those thirty extra pounds, or get everything perfect, or this or that comes into my life . . . then I will have ME." What if YOU are literally the active ingredient that makes everything work? This reality is like a trap door in a house of mirrors of judgments and conclusions, which are all lies. If you try to make one of those lies true, you take one step in and then keep trying to look for all the other lies to validate the first one. You will keep trying to see what's true and how everybody else is doing it. Then you're stuck trying to find the validity and truth in what was never true in the first place.

This reality is like a Pinto® that is broken down. It doesn't run and it is stuck on the side of the road waiting for a tow truck to take it to the dump. You, as the infinite being you are, can make anything run. So you jump in, and you're flying forty mph on the freeway while bumpers and tires are flying off and you're so infinite it doesn't stop you. Except you can't go more than 40 mph, and every time you turn around something is going wrong. That's because the Pinto® doesn't run without you. You are the gas that makes the Pinto® run. The only reason why anything in this reality has given you more of you, was because you were choosing you. Would you like to just pull over and get out of the Pinto® and receive that you are actually a beautiful Ferrari® that flies through life with ease?

The only time this reality works to give you more of you is when you are choosing for you. Recall a time in your life when you chose to have something in your life, like a relationship or more money. You received the money and felt like, "Ahhh, I feel like I have more of me," because you could buy things you like or take a nice vacation. What if the reason why you felt like you had more of you wasn't about the money? What if your choice to receive more of you was what gave you more of you? Or you got into a relationship and felt like it gave you more of you. What if your choice to open your heart and receive you gave you more of you, not the relationship? What if it's never about the "thing" and always about the energy? Based on this reality, you thought it was the money, or the relationship that was giving you more of you. Instead, it was you simply choosing to have more of you that gave you more of you. What if the money and relationship were the by-product of you choosing more of you?

Everything that you've been doing to eternally search for more of you in all the constructs of this reality, will you destroy and un-create all that?
Right, Wrong, Good, Bad, POC, POD, All 9, Shorts, Boys and Beyonds™.

Imagine if this was on the nightly news ... SPECIAL URGENT NEWS FLASH ... You are the catalyst for what is working in your life. You are the gas in the Pinto®. You are the secret ingredient that makes everything work.

When you are choosing 100% for you, no matter what, 100% of your life will be greater than anything you can even imagine! You can ask, "If I were doing this all for me, what energy would I be?" When you begin to step into this awareness you become like the Mama duck, and you have all these little baby ducks, called everything you desire in your life, and they are all following you. If you choose 100% for you, you'll turn around and find you've got a great relationship and money, a great business and all of these wonderful people in your life, and they just follow you because you are always choosing for you.

Everything you have been unwilling to be, know, perceive and receive about that, will you destroy and un-create it?
Right, Wrong, Good, Bad, POC, POD, All 9, Shorts, Boys and Beyonds™.

It's interesting, because you have been using this system (this reality) that doesn't work, and it's not meant to work. It works for creating destruction, for killing your body, for creating separation in relationships, for eliminating you from your life and it works for making your life heavy. It doesn't work for you. It never has. Yet, choosing for you actually does work.

What are you going to think about you if your life isn't working for you? That YOU don't work? What if it's not that you don't work? What if this reality doesn't work? It's almost like this reality gets you to continually point to the perpetual wrongness of you, instead of the awareness that it doesn't work. For example, have you ever met the man or woman of your dreams and felt like you were having more of you? But, you're using this realities' tools in the creation of that relationship. So you meet, and it's wonderful beyond your wildest imagination. Then you conclude, "We're going to be together forever!" Then you make commitments to never receive from anyone else. You make them significant and give up your life. You create judgments about who they are and who you are for them. What happens to the "man or woman of your dreams" energy in the relationship? Was there more energy in the beginning or after a few years of that? More energy in the beginning, huh? When it doesn't work, you then think that somehow you don't work, that there is something wrong with you, instead of knowing this reality doesn't work. Then go to the eternal wrongness of you as if it's true. What if the part of the relationship that gave you more of you, was your choice to receive more of you?

Except, here you are, driving this old beat-up Pinto®. YOU are the infinite, gold gas that even gets the Pinto® to run in the first place! YOU are this heavenly, generative energy, space and consciousness. You can drive anything. You can get a Pinto® to run at three hundred miles per hour! How powerful are you? If you were choosing your life for you, you'd be flying like a Ferrari® at light speed. But you keep trying to drive this reality as if it's because of you that you can only go three hundred miles per hour.

It's what we call the Kingdom of Crapdom, everywhere you've been trying to make this reality work. Let's just keep working on all this stuff that is wrong with me, because I am the problem. It's not that I am in the house of the Kingdom of Crapdom, but I am the problem. What if you are not the common denominator that screws everything up in your life? What if the judgment and conclusion reality is the common denominator that has screwed anything up in your life?

Everything that brings up, everywhere you have made you the wrongness, problem or common denominator for what isn't working in your life, when what isn't working is anywhere you've installed or imported this reality, will you destroy and un-create it all?
Right, Wrong, Good, Bad, POC, POD, All 9, Shorts, Boys and Beyonds™.

You know how when there is a truth with a lie attached, it feels a little confusing? Things still work, but not totally. Have you ever studied the Law of Attraction? The basic principles being, whatever you put out there you attract. It's somewhat true, and somewhat not. The true part is the energy you choose to be and receive does dictate what the Universe can gift to you. The lie is that you attract everything. Say you are walking down the street and pass a drunken homeless person. Then you think, wow, there is something about me that is attracting a homeless person. What's wrong with me? What do I still need to work on, because I must be attracting it? How am I still functioning as a drunk? Even if the truth is you don't drink, you would still be making yourself accountable for what you "attracted." When you combine a truth and a lie it can really screw you up, because it works sometimes, but not all the time. When it doesn't work you think YOU are the one that is wrong.

Everything that brings up, everywhere you've made yourself wrong and think that you don't work when it's the lie that doesn't work, will you destroy and un-create it all? Right, Wrong, Good, Bad, POC, POD, All 9, Shorts, Boys and Beyonds™.

What if that is the same for the judgment and conclusion reality? You keep trying to use it because you feel like sometimes it works. It feels heavy and light at the same time. Guess what is the truth about what works in this reality? YOU. You are the active ingredient in this reality that makes it work at all. If we choose for the infinite beings we truly be, the structure of this reality would begin to cease to exist. In the judgment and conclusion reality, when you stop functioning from it, it doesn't exist for you. What if everything that hasn't worked in your life was based on where you were functioning from this reality?

Everything that brings up, will you destroy and un-create it all? Right, Wrong, Good, Bad, POC, POD, All 9, Shorts, Boys and Beyonds™.

What if you embraced the awareness . . . "Oh my goodness! I've always worked! I'm the thing that works! There is nothing wrong with me! The only time my life hasn't worked is when I was choosing based on this reality and not my choice for me!"

KEY INDICATORS THAT YOU ARE DRIVING A PINTO®

If you are choosing based on . . . .

- Where you fit.
- What you're going to benefit.
- What you're going to win.
- What you're going to lose, or not going to lose.
- If you're striving for perfection.
- If you're trying to be "right."
- If you trying not to be "wrong."
- If you're trying to make someone else "right" or "wrong."
- If you think something or someone will give you more of you.
- If you're searching for validation.
- If you're making something or someone significant.

- If you're resisting or reacting or aligning and agreeing.
- If you're making anything or anyone greater than you.
- If you're in any judgment or conclusion.
- If you're trying to control.
- If you're proving you are not something (you actually believe that you are it).
- If you're proving you are something (you actually believe that you are not it).
- If you take any point of view.
- If you're vested in the outcome.
- If you want anything for anyone.
- If you ever say, "If I just had this, then my life would be okay."
- If you're fighting for your freedom (You actually believe you're not free).
- If you're trying to make someone else happy.
- If you're controlling anything.
- If you expect anything from anyone.
- If you're doing worry, guilt, fear, regret, blame, or shame.
- Choosing based on what is comfortable.
- Avoiding the uncomfortable.

None of these will ever give you more of you. They are all trap doors that lead to more of this reality.
Only you can give you, you.

Today I would like to introduce to you a new concept that you can use to begin to unravel all of the limitations from every lifetime called "secret agendas." Every judgment and conclusion you've made from any lifetime becomes a secret agenda. Do you remember every point of view you've taken from your childhood and every lifetime? No, huh? You might remember pictures or flashes of memories but every point of view? All of these points of view from every lifetime become the secret agendas that are running your life today. These secret agendas are what create reaction instead of choice, answer instead of question, and conclusions instead of possibilities.
You can fill in the blanks to begin changing any area of your life.

What secret agenda with _____ am I using to maintain and entrain

_____ ?

Everything that brings up, will you destroy and un-create it all?
Right, Wrong, Good, Bad, POC, POD, All 9, Shorts, Boys and Beyonds™.

We say, "maintain" because you actually have to maintain your limitations. If you stopped planting, watering, and "maintaining" your limitations they would cease to exist. The word "entrain" is where you have adjusted your vibration to be in sync with another. You have entrained you to the vibrations of your parents, your culture, your friends, your poverty, your judgments of you . . . etcetera.

HERE'S AN EXAMPLE:

What secret agenda with money do I have that maintains and entrains the rightness of only having enough to get by?
Everything that brings up, will you destroy and un-create it all?
Right, Wrong, Good, Bad, POC and POD, All 9, Shorts, Boys and Beyonds

What secret agenda with my body do I have that maintains and entrains the proof of everything I think is wrong with me and my life?
Everything that brings up will you destroy and un-create all that?
Right, Wrong, Good, Bad, POC, POD, All 9, Shorts, Boys and Beyonds™.

Fill in the blanks to begin unlocking all the secret agendas that are running your life.

What secret agenda with _____ am I using to maintain and entrain
_____?
Everything that brings up, will you destroy and un-create it all?
Right, Wrong, Good, Bad, POC, POD, All 9, Shorts, Boys and Beyonds™.

What secret agenda with _____ am I using to maintain and entrain
_____?

Everything that brings up, will you destroy and un-create it all?
Right, Wrong, Good, Bad, POC, POD, All 9, Shorts, Boys and Beyonds™.

What secret agenda with _____ am I using to maintain and entrain
_____?

Everything that brings up, will you destroy and un-create it all?
Right, Wrong, Good, Bad, POC, POD, All 9, Shorts, Boys and Beyonds™.

What secret agenda with _____ am I using to maintain and entrain
_____?

Everything that brings up, will you destroy and un-create it all?
Right, Wrong, Good, Bad, POC, POD, All 9, Shorts, Boys and Beyonds™.

What secret agenda with _____ am I using to maintain and entrain
_____ _?

Everything that brings up, will you destroy and un-create it all?
Right, Wrong, Good, Bad, POC, POD, All 9, Shorts, Boys and Beyonds™.

What secret agenda with _____ am I using to maintain and entrain
_____ ?

Everything that brings up, will you destroy and un-create it all?
Right, Wrong, Good, Bad, POC, POD, All 9, Shorts, Boys and Beyonds™.

What secret agenda with _____ am I using to maintain and entrain
_____ ?

Everything that brings up, will you destroy and un-create it all?
Right, Wrong, Good, Bad, POC, POD, All 9, Shorts, Boys and Beyonds™.

What secret agenda with _____ am I using to maintain and entrain
_____ ?

Everything that brings up, will you destroy and un-create it all?
Right, Wrong, Good, Bad, POC, POD, All 9, Shorts, Boys and Beyonds™.

What secret agenda with _____ am I using to maintain and entrain
_____ ?

Everything that brings up, will you destroy and un-create it all?
Right, Wrong, Good, Bad, POC, POD, All 9, Shorts, Boys and Beyonds™.

What secret agenda with _____ am I using to maintain and entrain
_____ ?

Everything that brings up, will you destroy and un-create it all?
Right, Wrong, Good, Bad, POC, POD, All 9, Shorts, Boys and Beyonds™.

What secret agenda with _____ am I using to maintain and entrain
_____ ?

Everything that brings up, will you destroy and un-create it all?
Right, Wrong, Good, Bad, POC, POD, All 9, Shorts, Boys and Beyonds™.

Now that we have stepped into the advanced processing section of the program I've started a section called . . . .

PROCESSES SOUP: Random recipes to set you free

What secret agenda with this reality do you have that maintains and entrains the eternal and perpetual wrongness of you, instead of the awareness that it wasn't meant to work?
Everything that brings up, will you destroy and un-create all that?
Right, Wrong, Good, Bad, POC, POD, All 9, Shorts, Boys and Beyonds™.

What secret agenda with the lie that you have to function from this reality as your reality are you using to maintain and entrain the eternal and perpetual wrongness of you as if you're the thing that doesn't work?
Everything that brings up, will you destroy and un-create all that?
Right, Wrong, Good, Bad, POC, POD, All 9, Shorts, Boys and Beyonds™.

What secret agenda with money do you have that maintains and entrains you never allowing you to receive you?
Everything that brings up, will you destroy and un-create all that?
Right, Wrong, Good, Bad, POC, POD, All 9, Shorts, Boys and Beyonds™.

What secret agenda with relationship do you have that maintains and entrains you never allowing you to have a nurturing, kind, caring, expansive, joyful, money-expanding and life-expanding relationship?
Everything that brings up, will you destroy and un-create all that?
Right, Wrong, Good, Bad, POC, POD, All 9, Shorts, Boys and Beyonds™.

What secret agenda with your body do you have that maintains and entrains you never allowing you to have a joyful, exuberant expression of abundance as conscious embodiment?
Everything that brings up, will you destroy and un-create all that?
Right, Wrong, Good, Bad, POC, POD, All 9, Shorts, Boys and Beyonds™.

Day 14 ❧ Secret of the Universe Daily Exercise

STEP 1: Pull over, and get out of the Pinto®. Just leave it on the side of the street, and function from the Ferrari® of light speed. Getting out of the judgment and conclusion reality and realizing you are the active ingredient that makes anything work will really change your life.

STEP 2: Begin running the clearing statement: "What secret agenda with_____ _____ am I using to maintain and entrain _____? This will begin unlocking all of the limitations you've created in any lifetime that are running your life.

NOTES: _____

_____

_____

_____

_____

_____

_____

_____

_____

_____

_____

_____

Stop . . . See you tomorrow!

Day 15

What if you are a Superhero and don't know it?

DAILY EXERCISE:
For today you are going to acknowledge the Superhero you truly be. After every interaction, stop for a minute and ask . . . "Okay, if I was a Superhero, what did I just do here?" Allow yourself to go beyond what you even think is possible, and over acknowledge yourself for everything.

What if you are really a dynamic wizard or Superhero with talents, abilities, and capacities beyond your wildest imagination?

Now that we've got you out of the Pinto® and into the Ferrari® you truly be, we can begin showing you just how to drive this amazing, talented, infinite being called you! Have you ever woke up in the morning and felt like you got hit by a Mack® truck? Have you ever spent time with someone and afterward feel so exhausted you have to go to sleep? You think, "Did anyone get the license plate of the Mack® truck that just hit me?"

Whenever this occurs you are being a Superhero and not acknowledging it. You can just ask . . . "What talents, abilities, and capacities am I unwilling to be aware of here?"

What if you are a Superhero, doing Superhero magical things all the time, except you don't allow yourself to be aware of it?

It's funny because you hide your cape, your wand, and all your Superhero capacities from yourself, and then wonder why you feel so exhausted. You are changing everything for everyone and facilitating more consciousness everywhere you go.

Everything you are unwilling to perceive, know, be and receive about that will you destroy and un-create it all?
Right, Wrong, Good, Bad, POC, POD, All 9, Shorts, Boys and Beyonds™.

NOTE: anytime you "feel" like saying, "I don't know," run, "everything I am unwilling to perceive, know, be and receive about this, Right, Wrong, Good, Bad, POC, POD, All 9, Shorts, Boys and Beyonds™" and whatever it is will become more clear to you.

List some of your Superhero talents, abilities and capacities below.

1._____

2._____

3._____

4._____

5._____

For this moment, can you just acknowledge yourself and the amazing, brilliant, infinite, huge gift you truly be?
Everything that doesn't allow that to show up, will you destroy and un-create it all?
Right, Wrong, Good, Bad, POC, POD, All 9, Shorts, Boys and Beyonds™.

In one of my classes this extraordinary, phenomenal being was expressing how she often would feel like someone beat her up energetically after spending time with people. When I began to ask her questions about it, she saw what was really occurring. She has an amazing capacity to heal dis-ease in other people's bodies. She wasn't willing to be aware of what was actually happening, so her body was letting her know by the Mack® truck energy to acknowledge her talent and abilities. See, your body speaks in a feather touch. When you don't listen, it's only option is to turn up the volume, which is what you call "pain."

How much of the "pain" that you feel in your body is your body trying to get you to claim, own, and acknowledge your talents, abilities and capacities?

Everything that doesn't allow you to perceive, know, be and receive them, will you destroy and un-create all that?
Right, Wrong, Good, Bad, POC, POD, All 9, Shorts, Boys and Beyonds™.

What if even talking with someone for a few minutes could change the course of their life? You might be getting your morning coffee and ask a person just one question that could unravel their limitation and set them free.

Everywhere you haven't been willing to perceive, know, be and receive the contribution you truly be, will you destroy and un-create it all?
Right, Wrong, Good, Bad, POC, POD, All 9, Shorts, Boys and Beyonds™.

Also, if you are unwilling to be aware of just how talented and amazing you truly are, would you allow yourself to receive more money? Everything that doesn't allow that will you destroy and un-create it all?

Right, Wrong, Good, Bad, POC, POD, All 9, Shorts, Boys and Beyonds™.

Ponder this . . . .

What percentage of your talents, abilities and capacities do you allow yourself to be aware of? _____% For instance, if you are a body worker and you only allow yourself to be aware of around _____% percent of your talents, abilities and capacities with bodies, are you going to feel comfortable asking for and receiving tons of money for your sessions? Not so much.

You probably wouldn't allow someone to pay you tons of money because from your point of view, there is no product. During your session you are only aware of _____% of what you are contributing, so why would someone pay you tons of money?

What if you allowed the Universe to pay you for the Superhero you truly be? Everything that doesn't allow that, will you destroy and un-create it all?

Right, Wrong, Good, Bad, POC, POD, All 9, Shorts, Boys and Beyonds™.

If you're only allowing yourself to perceive, know, be and receive 3% of your talents, abilities, and capacities, you are using 97% of your energy to facilitate miracles of which you're not willing to be aware. Doesn't it make sense that not being aware of those miracles would feel like the energy of tired beyond belief?

So with this awareness of only acknowledging 3% of you, you are walking around the world being aware of everybody else and thinking you are that awareness. Since you only allow yourself to have 3% of who you truly be, the world around you fills in that 97%. This is one of the elements that has you being affected by the world around you. What if you are not your awareness? What if you increased your awareness of you to 100% of you, so that you know that none of the heaviness belonged to you?

For example, let's say you have dinner with someone and just over a simple conversation you ask a few key questions and change the whole trajectory of their future. Before you asked these questions they were headed towards poverty, and now they are going to be a super successful business person. If you really acknowledged the gift you were in that person's life, how much would that change your life and your receiving of you? You would then allow the Universe to pay you in all kinds of ways from all directions because you would actually be receiving the gift that you truly be.

Everything that doesn't allow that will you destroy and un-create it all?
Right, Wrong, Good, Bad, POC, POD, All 9, Shorts, Boys and Beyonds™.

So when you feel like you got "hit by a Mack® truck," it is kind of like the Universe and your body asking you to see just what a gift and contribution you really are. When you are willing to be totally conscious and aware of all the talents, abilities and capacities, does it make sense that it would be easy to have your talents, abilities and capacities?

Everywhere you have robbed yourself for an eternity of being, knowing, perceiving, and receiving the magnificent, talented, amazing, infinite being you truly be in totality, will you now destroy and un-create it all? Everything that brings up will you destroy and un-create it all now?
Right, Wrong, Good, Bad, POC, POD, All 9, Shorts, Boys and Beyonds™.

What amazing talents, abilities and capacities do you have that are outside of everything you think is possible?
Everything that doesn't allow you to perceive, know be and receive them will you destroy and un-create it all?
Right, Wrong, Good, Bad, POC, POD, All 9, Shorts, Boys and Beyonds™.

NOTE: You have every talent, ability and capacity. You are a being that changes the world. The change is the gift. You being is the talent, ability and capacity. It doesn't matter what vehicle you're driving at the moment; presenting for a group, hugging your child, loving your partner, singing or dancing. Everywhere you show up as you, you change the world.

With every interaction you can allow yourself to receive the awareness of how your Superhero talents, abilities and capacities are changing the world.

You are a gift to the world.

You are a gift to you.

You are a gift to everyone around you.

If you actually acknowledged what a gift you truly be, would you ever make yourself wrong or judge you, or be unhappy or sad about you? Or after every interaction would you think, "Wow, how cool am I? Did you see what I just facilitated for them? Do you see how different their future is? Do you see the healing I did on their body? How did I get so lucky to be me today?"

From your point of view if you "over acknowledged" you, what percentage of the contribution you truly be would you actually be acknowledging? _____%

Now expand out as big as the Universe and allow yourself to perceive, know, be and receive you as the infinite being that is oneness and consciousness of all things . . . Ask the Universe now . . . .

What percentage of you were you actually acknowledging? _____%

What if it was time to truly acknowledge the infinite being you truly be?

Hint for all Superheros . . . You are the oneness and consciousness of all things. You are far more talented and amazing then you have ever given yourself credit. It's time for you to know who you truly are.

Everything you have been doing to create walls of separation from you and all your talents, abilities and capacities, will you destroy and un-create it all? Right, Wrong, Good, Bad, POC, POD, All 9, Shorts, Boys and Beyonds™.

A lot of people won't allow themselves to acknowledge the greatness they are because they don't want to do superiority or make others feel inferior. What if you being the greatness you be was their only chance to have a different possibility? If you don't show up as you, you are robbing them from the greatness they truly be? Would you allow your greatness to shine its radiant light?

Also, have you ever heard someone gloating about how great they are? That person is telling everyone "I'm great. I'm so great. Look at how great I am!" Do they actually know they're great, or is their real point of view that they are terrible? When you know you are great you have no need to tell anyone about it. You have kept yourself from knowing how great you are because you don't want to be that ugly energy. When you have all of you, you are being greatness. Your level of having the oneness and consciousness of all things is superior to others. You are being superior not doing superior. What if superior wasn't a judgment? If there is a new BMW® and a VW® bug from 1970, which one is the superior car? Which one can accelerate faster? The new BMW,® huh? All the judgments you have about being superior, will you destroy and un-create all that? A lot of people will fight this awareness and say "everyone is created equal." Yes, created equal, and what choices have they made since then?

Everything you have been doing to avoid being superior which would keep you from being, knowing, perceiving, and receiving the real you, will you destroy and un-create it all? Right, Wrong, Good, Bad, POC, POD, All 9, Shorts, Boys and Beyonds™.

Also, as you begin to have an awareness of just how amazing, talented and phenomenal you truly are, you don't have to tell anyone. For the most part, people are not willing to have this awareness. So if you tell someone what they are not willing to receive, they will throw it back at you with daggers attached. Have you for you, and only tell people what they can hear.

Bonus: Secret of the Universe
Has anyone ever accused you of anything? Guess what, people will accuse you of what they themselves are doing. So everywhere anyone has accused you of anything and you thought it had anything to do with you, will you destroy and un-create it all? Right, Wrong, Good, Bad, POC, POD, All 9, Shorts, Boys and Beyonds™.

Processes Soup: Random recipes to set you free
What secret agenda with never acknowledging your talents and abilities, and what's really going on do you have, that maintains and entrains the lack of receiving you have in your life?
Everything that brings up will you destroy and un-create all that?
Right, Wrong, Good, Bad, POC, POD, All 9, Shorts, Boys and Beyonds™.

What secret agenda with never acknowledging you and your talents and abilities, and the phenomenal being of change you be, are you using in order to maintain and entrain the lack of receiving in your life? Everything that brings up, will you destroy and un-create it all?
Right, Wrong, Good, Bad, POC, POD, All 9, Shorts, Boys and Beyonds™.

What secret agenda with the oaths, vows, swearings, commitments, comealties and fealties to never perceive know be and receive your talents and abilities to everything you truly be do you have that maintains and entrains the lack of receiving you in your life? Everything that brings up, will you destroy and un-create it all?
Right, Wrong, Good, Bad, POC, POD, All 9, Shorts, Boys and Beyonds™.

Fealty is an oath to a liege or lord whom you have decided is greater than you.
Comealty is a fealty and commitment married into our physical structure; it's a fealty mingled within our blood.

How many oaths, vows, swearings, commitments, comealties, fealties do you have to never ever be, know, perceive and receive you ever again?
Everything that brings up, will you destroy and un-create it all?
Right, Wrong, Good, Bad, POC, POD, All 9, Shorts, Boys and Beyonds™.

What secret agenda with always hiding in your character, costume, role and contribution of you as Clark Kent are you using to maintain and entrain never allowing you to perceive, know, be or receive the Superhero you truly be? Everything that brings up, will you destroy and un-create it all?
Right, Wrong, Good, Bad, POC, POD, All 9, Shorts, Boys and Beyonds™.

Day 15 ∾ Secret of the Universe Daily Exercise

Today you are a Superhero, so put on that cape you hide in your closet! For today you are going to acknowledge the Superhero you truly be. After every interaction, cell phone call, even if you just read an e-mail, stop for a minute and ask . . . "Okay, If I was a Superhero, what did I just do here?" Then allow yourself to go beyond what you even think is possible, and over acknowledge yourself for everything. As if the wildest, most amazing, unbelievable change has just taken place. And then you can run the clearing statement . . . Everything that doesn't allow me to perceive, know, be and receive it, I will destroy and un-create it all. Right, Wrong, Good, Bad, POC, POD, All 9, Shorts, Boys and Beyonds™.

NOTES: _____

_____

_____

_____

_____

_____

_____

_____

_____

_____

Stop . . . See you tomorrow!

Day 16

Choosing your life in 10 second increments, being in total allowance and letting go of control

DAILY EXERCISE:
For today be in total allowance of everything. If you find you are resisting or reacting or aligning and agreeing with anything run, "Everything I am resisting or reacting or aligning and agreeing with here, I will destroy and un-create. Right, Wrong, Good, Bad, POC, POD, All 9, Shorts, Boys and Beyonds™." Ask yourself, "Am I doing control or allowance here?"

Would you like to know how to be free from every limitation and your past in its entirety? This is one of the biggest keys to the kingdom and doorways to infinite choice and infinite possibility. Be in allowance. Allowance means you never resist or react or align and agree with anything and you will not be affected, influenced or controlled by it.

What if you were in allowance of your childhood in its entirety?
Everything you have resisted or reacted to or aligned and agreed with that is controlling you, will you destroy and un-create it all?
Right, Wrong, Good, Bad, POC, POD, All 9, Shorts, Boys and Beyonds™.

Prior to knowing that total allowance is your doorway out of everything, you would create all kinds of resistance, reaction, alignment and agreement and in the attempt to be free twist it all out of your Universe. Have you ever been in a relationship with someone and they said something that really hurt your feelings? Like, "You might want to work out more." The energy behind what they said was mean and judgmental. They had judgments of your body and of you. They thought you weren't attractive anymore. When they said, "You might want to work out more." Did it mean so much to you that it hurt? At that point if you want to stay in love with that person you would try to make what they said "meaningless" to you, even if it meant everything from your point of view. You would then twist everything that meant so much to you out of your Universe so that you could stay with them. What that creates is an explosive button for your future. Someone in a future relationship then says, "Hey, wanna go work out?" with no judgment behind it, and you instantaneously turn into an emotional mess wondering what is wrong with you that you are so sensitive in this area. That's what happens when you make something meaningless. The real keys to the kingdom are undoing all the resistance, reaction, alignment and agreement from your past to be in total allowance of it, instead of making it meaningless and twisting it out of your Universe. If emotional reaction ever occurs in your life, run, "Everything I have made meaningless about this in any lifetime that actually meant everything to me I will destroy and un-create it all. Right, Wrong, Good, Bad, POC, POD, All 9, Shorts, Boys and Beyonds™."

You as an infinite being are as big as the Universe and beyond. From that space you are in total allowance of everything and every molecule. There is no existence of resistance, reacting, judging, aligning, agreeing, and no conclusions about anything, just infinite space. When you be that infinite space and allowance, you can choose anything and magic happens around you all the time. When you be that energy, space and consciousness of total allowance, you change the world just by being.

When you align, agree, react, resist, conclude or judge, it creates a contraction in your Universe. It is from the space of expansion that you have true infinite choice. How often do you think you need to judge or conclude something to make a choice? Or you try and weigh out the pros and cons of the particular choice. All of that is actually the elimination of choice, not true choice. What if you chose from the infinite menu of choice? What if you chose from a space of total caring, total allowance and infinite possibility in 10 second increments?

Are you a control freak of magnitude? There are two types of control; controlling from conclusion, and controlling from question, choice and contribution. Let's talk about controlling from conclusion. Controlling from conclusion is when you are coming from a point of view, or invested in the result or outcome.

• Control, would that be receiving or not receiving? Not receiving.
• Control, would that be question or conclusion? Conclusion.
• Control, would that be the space of no judgment or total judgment? Total judgment.
• Control, would that be total allowance or not being in allowance? Not allowance.

If you think about the energy of control, it feels like a contraction, right? There are judgments and conclusions around the control. What if your attempt to control things in your life was limiting the infinite ways the Universe could gift to you? You cannot control and receive at the same time. If you were allowing yourself to infinitely receive, would you be able to function from control? What if you became "out of control" with receiving?

Everything that doesn't allow that, will you destroy and un-create it all?
Right, Wrong, Good, Bad, POC, POD, All 9, Shorts, Boys and Beyonds™.

Also, if you had no conclusions, is there anything to control? Would you be willing to give up your status of control freak of the Universe?

Everything that doesn't allow that, will you destroy and un-create it all?
Right, Wrong, Good, Bad, POC, POD, All 9, Shorts, Boys and Beyonds™.

What if you allowed yourself to choose just for you, just for fun? Then you would never have to judge or conclude before you made a choice.

Would you be willing to give up control and find out what it would be like to have a life of allowance of everything and choose from there?
Everything that doesn't allow that, will you destroy and un-create it all?
Right, Wrong, Good, Bad, POC, POD, All 9, Shorts, Boys and Beyonds™.

Look at the energy of your life if you are controlling everything into existence and you have all kinds of conclusions about what you want. Then something doesn't go as you wanted, and there is all kinds of trauma and drama about it not working. Then you try and manipulate everyone and everything back into what your conclusions were. Since every conclusion is a limitation, you are controlling your life to be limited. Is there any room for the Universe to gift you with something greater than anything you can currently imagine? No. Anytime you are trying to control are you creating the opposite result? It's like driving a Pinto® in the wrong direction wondering why you're not getting where you would like to go. When it doesn't work, then you go to the wrongness of you. Did you know the road the Pinto® drives on only leads to the wrongness of you?

Everything that doesn't allow that, will you destroy and un-create it all?
Right, Wrong, Good, Bad, POC, POD, All 9, Shorts, Boys and Beyonds™.

Now, look at the energy of your life where you are in absolute allowance of every molecule to choose whatever it desires. Where you can make choices from infinite space, infinite caring, where everything turns out greater than anything you could have imagined or planned. Look at the space of caring and gratitude for your life when you are in allowance of every molecule to be anything and everything that it is. Which one feels more like the life that you would like to have?
What generative energy, space and consciousness can you and your body be that would allow you and your body to be in allowance of every molecule in the entire Universe to be exactly as it is?

One time I was hosting a class for Dr. Dain Heer and I was literally controlling everyone into choosing to take the class. Then, two days before the class, I felt like throwing up, my bones and joints hurt, and my whole body hurt. I called Dain and asked him what was going on. He said, "Are you just a little invested on who shows up for this class?" and I said "Yes, I am controlling the whole Universe in showing up." He asked "So, how does your body feel about that?" Obviously, my body didn't like it. My body was sending me the message to let them choose for themselves. Once I was aware of this, all of my symptoms went away. Sometimes people need to create a level of disaster before they choose consciousness. If you try to control them out of the disaster you see coming for them, you rob them of all of the information they require in order to finally choose for them. Only if they choose for them, is their life going to work for them.

Control affects every element of your life totally. If you are invested in controlling into conclusion you also have to do all kinds of anti-consciousness, and your life and body are going to reflect it. Think about a person in your life that you really, really, really want them to choose something different. What percentage of your energy are you using in order to get them to choose something different? How much manipulating and control do you have to do in order to get them to choose what you want them to?

All the energy from your body that you have been using to try and get someone else to choose something different, would you now destroy and un-create all that? Right, Wrong, Good, Bad, POC, POD, All 9, Shorts, Boys and Beyonds™.

How many of you do control to prove how potent you are? We talk about potency instead of power in Access Consciousness™ because for the most part power in this reality is power over others. Anywhere you are proving anything you believe the opposite. So your underlying point of view is that you believe you are not potent, so you keep proving to yourself how potent you are.

Everywhere you are controlling and creating challenges to prove how potent you are instead of knowing how potent you are, will you destroy and un-create all that? Right, Wrong, Good, Bad, POC, POD, All 9, Shorts, Boys and Beyonds™.

Do you know how potent you have to be in order to drive a Pinto® and keep it running? Everything in this Pinto® breaks down in every moment and you keep holding it all together. What if you are far more potent then you've ever given yourself credit for?

Everything that doesn't allow you to perceive, know, be and receive that will you destroy and un-create it all? Right, Wrong, Good, Bad, POC, POD, All 9, Shorts, Boys and Beyonds™.

When you are controlling, you are forcing everyone into a "my-way" or the "highway" position. People can either choose to get on your boat and go where you're going or they fall off. If you're functioning from conclusion on the way down you energetically kick them. "Fine, get off my boat. I'm going the right direction and you should be going my direction or you're wrong!" This creates separation and they probably won't get back on your boat. Instead, what if you allowed them to go for a swim and get back on your boat if they choose? Who made you God? What if you let everyone have their choice? The key to the kingdom that unlocks the doorway for change is just being the infinite space of caring, gratitude and total allowance.

Has anyone ever really, really, really wanted you to choose something? Did it make you want to choose it more or less? Less. When you "want" something for someone and try to control them into choosing it, it creates the opposite result.

What people think is that if they were in total allowance they would be a doormat and everyone would walk all over them. Except, if you actually pair allowance with choice you will have infinite possibility and infinite energy available to you. Until you begin to allow yourself to choose from infinite space you will always create limitation.

Everywhere you think you have to take a point of view in order to not get walked on by every body else's points of view, will you destroy and un-create all that? Right, Wrong, Good, Bad, POC, POD, All 9, Shorts, Boys and Beyonds™.

How do you know that you are being in choice verses control? Anytime you have a point of view behind a choice, you are controlling. If you see a parking spot and think, "I'm getting that parking spot no matter what!" You will be upset if you don't get it. If you think "What would it take for a parking spot to show up?" You are allowing anything to happen, and will celebrate your parking spot if the Universe provides it. So by being in allowance and being in the question you allow magic to show up, but if you don't get that parking spot you're not upset and you're not making yourself wrong. Whenever you are vested in the outcome or doing control at all, you'll end up in the place of destruction and making yourself wrong if it doesn't work out the way you had planned.

So everything that brings up and everywhere you instituted so much control that everything either upsets you or you're trying to wrangle it into some conclusion that is making your life not so fun to be in, will you destroy and un-create all that? Right, Wrong, Good, Bad, POC, POD, All 9, Shorts, Boys and Beyonds™.

Day 16 ⁊ Secret of the Universe Daily Exercise

STEP 1: Be in total allowance of every molecule in the Universe. Anytime you feel yourself agreeing, aligning, resisting, reacting, controlling, creating judgment or concluding, run, "Everything I am resisting or reacting to or aligning and agreeing with I will destroy and un-create all that. Right, Wrong, Good, Bad, POC, POD, All 9, Shorts, Boys and Beyonds™."

STEP 2: Use everything that comes up today to POC and POD yourself until you are in total allowance of everything. Keep expanded out as big as the Universe and beyond. If you feel yourself contract at all ask, "Am I doing allowance or am I doing control here?" Everything that brings up, Right, Wrong, Good, Bad, POC, POD, All 9, Shorts, Boys and Beyonds™.

NOTES: _____

_____

_____

_____

_____

_____

_____

_____

_____

_____

_____

_____

Stop ... See you tomorrow!

Day 17

Contributing to You

DAILY EXERCISE:
For today stop controlling from conclusion, be in allowance of everyone and everything, and begin contributing to you.

The first step in having everything you would like to have in your life is giving up control and being in total allowance of everyone and everything to be exactly as it is. Once you are not vested in any outcome and are in total allowance, it opens up the space where you can begin contributing to you, your body and your life.

This is counter intuitive to most people in the creation of what they would like to have in their lives. Think about it. If you would like to have more money in your life, will you try and control everyone into giving you more money? Look at the energy of how that "feels." Have you ever walked by a vendor who tried to get you to buy his product? Were you invited to give him money or repulsed by the manipulative ways he was trying to control you? Every ounce of control is a repulsion from receiving and creates the opposite result energetically. It's like driving a Pinto® in the wrong direction and wondering why you're not getting where you want to go.

Everything that brings up, will you destroy and un-create all that?
Right, Wrong, Good, Bad, POC, POD, All 9, Shorts, Boys and Beyonds™.

If control has the opposite result of what you were desiring, then why spend anymore of your precious energy doing it? The only part about control that will work, is if you are in the equation, and this is just because you work.

One of my beautiful clients was telling me how she was working with these tools and doing great until she received a phone call from a friend. Her friend was going on and on about how she didn't have enough money and how hard life is and all of that fun stuff. My client was aware that this friend spends absolutely every dime she gets before she even gets it, and really didn't want to spend her time talking about how hard life is.

She was thinking to herself, well, if you didn't spend all of your money, you might have some! Of course, she didn't say these things out loud, she just got more and more annoyed and angry with her friend and by the time she hung up, she was in a bad mood.

This story from my client makes sense to most of us, because for the majority of our lives, we have not been in allowance and created us as affected by the world around us. What if you didn't have to be at the affect of the world around you? You could just breeze through interactions and life like it was a fun, receiving adventurous gift. The first step to that is allowance. The second step is, "What contribution can I be to me and my body here?"

My client was twisted up in knots by the time she hung up the phone for several reasons. First of all, she was in judgment of her friend for the way she chose to spend her money and not save any of it. Second, she was in conclusion that her friend was always going to choose that. Third, she was upset that her friend had brought her down when she felt great before the phone call.

You cannot be at the affect of anything, unless you choose to be. She chose to be at the affect of her friend by not being in allowance and not choosing to energetically contribute to her. You can choose to react, resist, align, agree, judge, conclude and limit. Or you can choose total allowance, infinite space, caring, and gratitude and ask, "What contribution can I be to me here?"

In that conversation, if she was being a contribution to herself, she could have said in her head, "Don't worry, body, she is choosing this because she loves it. There is nothing to take away from her here. How about we let her choose everything she's choosing? Expand out. Good, that's better." If she would have stepped into being a contribution to her, this phone conversation wouldn't have left her feeling twisted up in knots.

What if the way to be a contribution to everyone else, is by being a contribution to you? Everything that you are unwilling to know, be, perceive, and receive that your contribution to you is a contribution to everyone else, will you destroy and un-create all that?
Right, Wrong, Good, Bad, POC, POD, All 9, Shorts, Boys and Beyonds™.

How much do you contribute energy to all sorts of things, including control, judgment, other people, their lives, and not to you? You have to contribute a ton of energy to maintain limitation. What if you used that energy to contribute to you and your life instead?

Everything that brings up will you destroy and un-create all that? Right, Wrong, Good, Bad, POC, POD, All 9, Shorts, Boys and Beyonds™.

Once you release all the resistance and reaction in your life, you will begin to be able to choose to be a contribution to you. Remember the Pinto® and the Ferrari®? To step into the Ferrari®, all that is required is total allowance and then asking . . . "What can I contribute to me here?"

Literally, as long as you are doing control and not being in total allowance, you can't begin being a contribution to you. If you are vested and trying to control a friend into choosing being happy, everything you say or do is always trying to get them to be happy, which is actually creating the opposite result. You won't even think about, "What contribution can I be to me here?" You will be distracted, reactive, and vested. What if the only way to change anyone was to be in total allowance of what they were choosing and be the example of another possibility?

LIST THREE WAYS YOU CAN CONTRIBUTE TO YOUR BODY TODAY

1._____

2._____

3._____

LIST THREE WAYS YOU CAN CONTRIBUTE TO YOUR BUSINESS OR MONEY FLOWS TODAY

1._____

2._____

3._____

LIST THREE WAYS YOU CAN CONTRIBUTE TO YOUR RELATIONSHIP WITH YOU TODAY

1._____

2._____

3._____

Contributing to you is something that is highly judged in this reality as a "bad thing." Except, if you're the creator of your life and you refuse to contribute to you, how much can you receive? Not much, huh? When you allow you and the entire Universe to contribute to you, you are being and receiving more than others are willing to be and receive. Therefore, people around you will judge you in order to create separation and not receive you. What are some of the judgments people may choose to create? They may judge you as selfish, self-centered, egotistical, narcissistic, full of yourself, stuck-up, conceited, all that and a bag of chips. "You just want your cake and you want to eat it, too. Yes! I've baked my cake, of course I would like to enjoy it! How many of you have eliminated contributing to you in order to avoid those judgments?

Everything that brings up, will you destroy and un-create all that?
Right, Wrong, Good, Bad, POC, POD, All 9, Shorts, Boys and Beyonds™.

In this reality if you are contributing the energy of joy, people ask, "What drug are you on that you're so happy?"

What if contributing to you was a contribution to the whole world?

Processes Soup: Random recipes to set you free

What secret agenda with control do you have that maintains and entrains the disasters of limitations, judgments and conclusions that continuously get validated all around you at all times?
Everything that brings up, will you destroy and un-create it all?
Right, Wrong, Good, Bad, POC, POD, All 9, Shorts, Boys and Beyonds™.

What secret agenda with conclusion do you have that maintains and entrains never having everything you desire out of life?
Everything that brings up, will you destroy and un-create it all?
Right, Wrong, Good, Bad, POC, POD, All 9, Shorts, Boys and Beyonds™.

What secret agenda with control do you have that maintains and entrains the outcome of the opposite result that you love to hate?
Everything that brings up, will you destroy and un-create it all?
Right, Wrong, Good, Bad, POC, POD, All 9, Shorts, Boys and Beyonds™.

What secret agenda with control do you have that maintains and entrains the perpetual and eternal proof that you don't work and that you're wrong?
Everything that brings up, will you destroy and un-create it all?
Right, Wrong, Good, Bad, POC, POD, All 9, Shorts, Boys and Beyonds™.

What secret agenda with controlling into conclusion do you have that maintains and entrains the proof, validation, experience and justification of the wrongness and badness and you don't work?
Everything that brings up, will you destroy and un-create it all?
Right, Wrong, Good, Bad, POC, POD, All 9, Shorts, Boys and Beyonds™.

Day 17 ✎ Secret of the Universe Daily Exercise

FIRST STEP: Get out of your own way: No control

For all the control freaks of magnitude, here you go! Here is a key to the kingdom for you . . . control has the opposite result. Let go of control, and begin to be an out-of-control, infinite receiving being of magnitude!

SECOND STEP: Be in allowance of everything. Run, "What generative energy, space and consciousness can I be to allow every molecule to be exactly what it is?"

If you find you are not in allowance, run the clearing statement, expand out and make yourself as big as the Universe. If you would like to get the most out of today, you can also put yourself in a position where you would go into a lot of resistance and reaction and alignment and agreement and POC and POD until you are in total allowance. (like a family dinner?).

THIRD STEP: Ask, "What generative energy, space and consciousness can I be to be a contribution to me and my body here?

What if stepping into this contribution-to-you piece allowed everything you desire to be delivered to you on a silver platter, the world to change around you, and you to be the Ferrari® you truly are?

NOTES: _____

_____

_____

_____

Stop . . . See you tomorrow!

Day 18

Creating a nurturing, caring, kind, expansive and joyful relationship with your body

DAILY EXERCISE:
Today you are going to create a new relationship with your body built from honoring, trusting, receiving, adoring and being grateful for your body. Ask your body about everything, listen to your body, talk to your body, and nurture your body.

Now that we have unraveled a good portion of your judgments and conclusions, we can now begin creating a different relationship with your body. Your body is a sensory organ and is like the whiskers on a cat. It is here to give you information, and is like your "cat's whiskers." It has "feelers" to all the energetic receiving of the entire Universe. Your body is going to continually give you information, and if you have any judgment or conclusion in your Universe you can't receive that information clearly.

Everything that doesn't allow that clear communication, will you destroy and un-create it all?
Right, Wrong, Good, Bad, POC, POD, All 9, Shorts, Boys and Beyonds™.

Every judgment and conclusion eliminates receiving, locks what you're judging in place and creates your experience in your body. If you judge any energy as "bad" you will create a "bad" experience in your body. All the judgments and lies of past experience that you have programmed and locked into your body, will you destroy and un-create all that?
Right, Wrong, Good, Bad, POC, POD, All 9, Shorts, Boys and Beyonds™.

HOW TO CREATE A COMMUNION WITH YOUR BODY

STEP 1: Stop judging your body.
STEP 2: Destroy and un-create all your judgments and conclusions about your body.

Step 3: Ask your body everything that concerns it.
Step 4: Listen and honor what your body is asking for.

What if you began asking your body about everything that involves it? You can ask . . . "Body, what do you desire to eat?" "Body, do you desire to go do that?" "Body, do you desire to have sex with this person?" Every molecule in the Universe functions from question, including our bodies. If you are not in question, you are out of alignment with your body. Would you be willing to be in the question with your body?

Everything that brings up, will you destroy and un-create it all?
Right, Wrong, Good, Bad, POC, POD, All 9, Shorts, Boys and Beyonds™.

What if your body became your best friend and greatest conscious facilitator? What if your body is more conscious then you are? Your body can take your hand and show you how you and your body can be an energetic contribution to each other. Your body can show you. But, if you have all sorts of judgments about your body, you will eliminate receiving from it because judgment eliminates receiving.

How often are you totally grateful for your body? How often do you show your body just how much you appreciate it? What if you loved and adored your body, just like you would a puppy or kitty? What if you allowed the energy of your body to be constantly expanding and receiving?

Create a new and different relationship with your body . . . .

Honor Your Body

Start by beginning to honor your body. Ask your body about everything that has to do with it, which is pretty much everything. If you honored your body, would you ever judge it? Would you ever punish it or exclude it from your choices? Or would you listen intently to everything it is saying to you so that you could be more conscious for it? If I was choosing what is honoring for my body here, what would I choose?"

Everything that doesn't allow that, will you destroy and un-create all that?
Right, Wrong, Good, Bad, POC, POD, All 9, Shorts, Boys and Beyonds™.

Have Gratitude for Your Body

Be grateful for your body. What if your body wasn't a pile of debris you carry around? What if your body was your best friend that is always there for you? What if your body was the space of caring and no judgment for you that is always there to show you who you truly are? Your body never judges you, no matter how crazy you are.

Everything you have been unwilling to perceive, know, be and receive about that, will you destroy and un-create it all?
Right, Wrong, Good, Bad, POC, POD, All 9, Shorts, Boys and Beyonds™.

Your body is always present. It doesn't know how to not be present. You go in and out of awareness with your body. Your body can be this wonderful gift that keeps you present and receiving in your life. It can be this magical thing that anytime you tap into, it you can receive it. Your body can remind you, "hey, don't focus on all those judgments and conclusions, feel the sun warm the skin on your back." Or "stop a second and truly take in the wind as it blows through. Feel it. Allow it. Receive it." Your body is a magical potion that you can tap into at any time and have anything you desire energetically.

Everything you have been unwilling to perceive, know, be and receive about that, will you destroy and un-create it all?
Right, Wrong, Good, Bad, POC, POD, All 9, Shorts, Boys and Beyonds™.

Be Vulnerable with Your Body

Vulnerability is to be as the open wound, that you are never putting up a barrier to receiving anything. Being vulnerable is being present with every molecule and receiving every molecule of the Universe. What if your body is not separate from the Universe, and is not separate from the Earth?

Everything you have been doing to not receive you as the living organism called the Earth, will you destroy and un-create it all?
Right, Wrong, Good, Bad, POC, POD, All 9, Shorts, Boys and Beyonds™.

Also, never make any energy you perceive significant. When you make nothing significant, the energy just flows through you, but when you make it significant, you lock it into your body and it takes longer to undo it.

So everywhere you've made any energy you perceive significant, will you destroy and un-create it all?
Right, Wrong, Good, Bad, POC, POD, All 9, Shorts, Boys and Beyonds™.

TRUST YOUR BODY

What if your body is more conscious then you are? What if your body could be your greatest conscious facilitator? What if you can trust your body? What if your body has just been fulfilling your every desire? What if your body has never betrayed you? What if it has always been on your side giving you all the information and energetic awareness that would allow you to be more conscious? Muscle test everything with your body, until you can have a clear communication.

Also, how many ideas do you have about what "feels like" you? How much of that information is definition, conclusion, and judgment? All of it? This book and program is going to change you. Don't try and go back to "you." The "you" you were no longer exists.

Every thought, feeling and emotion that you have defined, "feels like you," will you destroy and un-create all that?
Right, Wrong, Good, Bad, POC, POD, All 9, Shorts, Boys and Beyonds™.

So everything that doesn't allow you to be the astronaut who discovers the new Galaxies of the space of no judgment for you, infinite caring, allowance, gratitude, and vulnerability for you and your body, will you destroy and un-create all that?
Right, Wrong, Good, Bad, POC, POD, All 9, Shorts, Boys and Beyonds™.

VIBRATIONAL VIRTUAL REALITIES

Everybody thinks that their experiences are fact and use their bodies to prove them right. Except, what is really occurring is people are creating judgments and conclusions and then experiencing their reality through the lens of those points of views or the vibrational virtual realities.

The vibrational virtual realties are like the holodeck in Star Trek®. You program in all these judgments and conclusions that create your life experience and think they are real and true and the way things are.

> *"Your point of view creates your reality, reality doesn't create your point of view."*
> —Dr. Dain Heer

You have complete choice in the "lens" from which you view the world. For example, if you judge and conclude your body is fat, your body will create a "fat" body in order to validate your reality. You will then see and receive the world through the idea that "you are fat." You also won't receive the energy that would change your body, because that would invalidate your point of view. What if your body is just being what you already decided it to be with every judgment you've taken? Everything you choose you will experience through those judgments. You will eat, but instead of enjoying and being grateful for every bite, you feel bad, guilty and think you're going to get fat which is telling your body to turn it into fat.

Everything that brings up, will you destroy and un-create all of it?
Right, Wrong, Good, Bad, POC, POD, All 9, Shorts, Boys and Beyonds™.

I used to be really affected by people who smoked pot. Basically this is how it works. I contrived a point of view that smoking pot was bad and wrong and I was right or conscious for not doing it. Then I went around my life and reality collecting evidence to make that point right and valid. Then I created pain in my throat and chest that was like being stabbed anytime I was around someone who was smoking pot. My body was validating my point of view. Its job is to do everything I ask it to, just like the Universe. It's doing everything it can to fulfill my every desire with every experience I am having, which I am using as the evidence to prove the rightness of my point of view. I will experience my life through all those vibrational virtual realities that aren't even real. After I let go of all of those points of view there is no "effect" in my body from people who are smoking pot around me. The "pain" of my throat and lungs being stabbed was my body asking "Please, let go of your points of view about this because it's not that much fun for me."

What vibrational virtual reality can you now destroy and un-create through which you've actually been experiencing your body, through that if you did, it would allow you to be in total communion with the entire Universe and your body?
Everything that brings up, will you destroy and un-create it all?
Right, Wrong, Good, Bad, POC, POD, All 9, Shorts, Boys and Beyonds™.

It's almost as if you use your body to prove that you are not powerful, that you don't have choice and that you don't want to be here, anyway. You then use all the experiences in your body though these vibrational virtual realities to prove that you were right in making that choice. What if you no longer had to be right?
Everything that does not allow that, will you destroy and un-create it all?
Right, Wrong, Good, Bad, POC, POD, All 9, Shorts, Boys and Beyonds™.

What if you found out that you were wrong about how wrong you were?

What if you found out that you were actually wrong about how right you were?

The other thing is you might feel like every time you pick up this book you get spacey. Yes! That's the point! We are letting go of all your limitations so that you can be the space of the entire Universe and choose anything you would like to have as your life. Your mind is like a chest of drawers. Whenever new information is introduced, you open all the chests of drawers to see where this new information validates your current reality. For most people when they can't figure out where to file it, they throw it out because it doesn't validate their limitations. It invalidates them.

You may feel angry or judgmental when listening to this new information. Anger comes up because you've been lying to you for an eternity. Judgments come up as an attempt to create separation and not receive the new information. So what if you began to receive all the information that would actually undo every limitation that you have stored in the filing cabinet called your logical mind? If your logical mind had all the answers to your life, wouldn't you have everything figured out by now?

Everything that brings up and everywhere you can now let your mind go as the leader of your life, will you destroy and un-create it all?
Right, Wrong, Good, Bad, POC, POD, All 9, Shorts, Boys and Beyonds™.

Is your body happy when you listen to your logical mind or when you listen to it?
Is the Universe really excited when you listen to your logical mind or when you listen to it?
What if you embraced the idea that every conclusion you have is just a limitation?

Everything that brings up and everything that you think is so right and so true, that is actually not allowing you to receive more, will you destroy and un-create it all?
Right, Wrong, Good, Bad, POC, POD, All 9, Shorts, Boys and Beyonds™.

A BIT ABOUT CHILDHOOD REALITIES . . . .

How much of people's adult lives do they spend, reliving their childhood conditioning, as if it was right, wrong, or even valuable? If you could remember all the judgments and conclusions you made before the age of two, you might be amazed at how your life is showing up just as you asked it to, when you were two.

How many points of view from your childhood are running your life right now?
Everything that brings up, will you destroy and un-create it all?
Right, Wrong, Good, Bad, POC, POD, All 9, Shorts, Boys and Beyonds™.

What if there is a way bigger Universe that would completely invalidate your entire childhood and your reality?

What if this bigger Universe is around you at all times attempting to break down all of those conclusions and judgments so that you can actually receive all that you desire?
Everything that does not allow that, will you destroy and un-create it all?
Right, Wrong, Good, Bad, POC, POD, All 9, Shorts, Boys and Beyonds™.

I had a client once who had developed a cancer in her body. I asked her, "for what reason are you creating this?" and, "what do you love about cancer?" At first she was angry at me for suggesting she would actually choose this, but after we peeled some layers. she revealed she had never felt her dad loved her, and she thought if she got sick enough, he would finally love her. I shared with her that I had chosen similar ideas in life as a child. I remember feeling unloved and uncared for at times and thinking to myself, "I'll just die. Then they will be sorry. Then they can just miss me and feel so bad for not loving me when I was alive."

Everything that brings up for you, will you destroy and un-create it all?
Right, Wrong, Good, Bad, POC, POD, All 9, Shorts, Boys and Beyonds™.

Everyone is actually creating their body and life with every point of view they hold. Your body is fulfilling your every request with every judgment and conclusion you take.

Everywhere you have used your body as proof that you absolutely have no choice about anything, because you wouldn't have the body you have if that were true, when your body was doing everything it could to give you everything for which you were asking, will you destroy and un-create all of that?
Right, Wrong, Good, Bad, POC, POD, All 9, Shorts, Boys and Beyonds™.

Do you experience "pain" with your body? Is pain real, or is pain a creation? Pain is an intensity of energy that you have decided is too intense for you to receive. Have you heard about mothers who have experienced labor and childbirth as a huge orgasm? What about those who also thought it was terribly painful? If you're experiencing pain, ask, "Body, what are you trying to tell me that I've been refusing to hear?" When you don't listen to your body its only way to get your attention is to turn up the volume. Also, sometimes people's bodies will create "pain" in order to get you to expand out as big as the Universe. Before having this information, if someone has pain in their bodies, they would cut off their awareness to their bodies. If you've cut off your awareness to your body's communication with you, does it make sense that your body would create bigger problems to get you to listen?

Everything that brings up, will you destroy and un-create all that?
Right, Wrong, Good, Bad, POC, POD, All 9, Shorts, Boys and Beyonds™.

Everything you have done to create your body from all the decisions, judgments, conclusions and computations from childhood (including in the womb), will you destroy and un-create all that?
Right, Wrong, Good, Bad, POC, POD, All 9, Shorts, Boys and Beyonds™.

PROCESSES SOUP: RANDOM RECIPES TO SET YOU FREE

What secret agenda with never being in allowance of you, do you have that maintains and entrains always resisting and reacting or aligning and agreeing with every other energy in order to control you into smallness, contraction and validation of everyone else's point of view? Everything that brings up, will you destroy and un-create it all?
Right, Wrong, Good, Bad, POC, POD, All 9, Shorts, Boys and Beyonds™

What secret agenda with allowance do you have that maintains and entrains never the ease, joy, glory, space, gratitude, allowance, caring, vulnerability, honoring and total trust of you?
Right, Wrong, Good, Bad, POC, POD, All 9, Shorts, Boys and Beyonds™

What creation of your bodies based solely and only on the vibrational virtual realities or VVRs of this reality, do you have that maintains and entrain your body as the evidential contrivance of your reality? Everything that brings up will you destroy and un-create it all?
Right, Wrong, Good, Bad, POC, POD, All 9, Shorts, Boys and Beyonds™.

What creation of your body do you have based solely and only on the VVR's of this reality, are you using in order to maintain and entrain the evidential contrivance of your reality as experienced through your body?
Right, Wrong, Good, Bad, POC, POD, All 9, Shorts, Boys and Beyonds™.

What secret agenda with the creation of your body do you have based solely and only through the VVR's of this reality, are you using in order to maintain and entrain the limitations, judgments and conclusions as a way to create finite embodiment?
Everything that brings up, will you destroy and un-create it all?
Right, Wrong, Good, Bad, POC, POD, All 9, Shorts, Boys and Beyonds™.

What secret agenda with the creation of your body as an evidential contrivance of your reality do you have that maintains and entrains the problems, diseases, illnesses, agings and contractions and limited embodiment you are currently experiencing? Everything that brings up, will you destroy and un-create it all? Right, Wrong, Good, Bad, POC, POD, All 9, Shorts, Boys and Beyonds™.

What creation of your body as the evidential contrivance of your reality do you have based solely and only through the VVR's of this reality, are you using to maintain and entrain the death, destruction, disorder, disease, weight, wrong image from your point of view, aging, oldings and disintegration of your body? Everything that brings up, will you destroy and un-create it all? Right, Wrong, Good, Bad, POC, POD, All 9, Shorts, Boys and Beyonds™.

What creation of your body as an evidential contrivance of your reality do you have based solely and only through the VVR's of this reality, are you using to maintain and entrain the judgment, the conclusion, the death, disorder, disease, aging, olding, disintegration and disentrainment of who, what, when, where, and how your body truly be's?

Right, Wrong, Good, Bad, POC, POD, All 9, Shorts, Boys and Beyonds™.

What creation of your body as the evidential contrivance of everyone else's reality are you using to maintain and entrain the body image, body design, body look, body feel, body energy, body vibration, body death, body disease, body disorder, body disintegration and body dysfunction you currently have? Right, Wrong, Good, Bad, POC, POD, All 9, Shorts, Boys and Beyonds™.

What secret agenda with the creation of your body as an evidential contrivance of everyone else's reality do you have based solely and only through the VVR's of this reality, are you using in order to maintain and entrain the body you love to hate? Right, Wrong, Good, Bad, POC, POD, All 9, Shorts, Boys and Beyonds™.

What secret agenda for the creation of you, your body, and your life do you have based solely and only through the VVR's of this realit,y are you using to maintain and entrain the wrongness of you in order to at least make your parents right? Everything that is, will you destroy and un-create it all? Right, Wrong, Good, Bad, POC, POD, All 9, Shorts, Boys and Beyonds™.

What secret agenda for the creation of you, your body, and your life in order to make your parents right so they don't feel so wrong about themselves based solely and only through the VVR's of this reality, do you have that maintains and entrains the body you love to hate, the money you do not allow yourself to have, the nurturing relationships that you continue to refuse, and the generative energy, space and consciousness as you that you continuously invalidate, eradicate, and eliminate with every judgment and conclusion you do? Everything that brings up, will you destroy and un-create it all?

Right, Wrong, Good, Bad, POC, POD, All 9, Shorts, Boys and Beyonds™.

Day 18 ❧ Secret of the Universe Daily Exercise

Begin developing a new relationship with your body. A relationship that is based on honoring, trusting, receiving, adoring and being grateful for your body. Ask your body about everything. Listen to your body. Talk to your body. Nurture your body. Based on all these clearings from this 21-day program you may be able to develop a relationship with your body from a different space.

QUESTION: "IF I WAS CHOOSING GRATITUDE FOR MY BODY . . . WHAT WOULD I CHOOSE?"

NOTES: _____

_____

_____

_____

_____

_____

_____

Stop . . . See you tomorrow! 🌱

Day 19

Choosing for your body in 10 second increments

DAILY EXERCISE:
Today we are going to explore choosing in 10 second increments for your body.
So you may wish to do this chapter on a day off. "If I had 10 seconds to choose
anything for my body what would I choose?"

Be totally present and choose for your body in 10 second increments.

What if you actually allowed yourself to be totally present with your body in 10 second
increments? This is one of the biggest keys to the kingdom.

You hear everything that is going on around you. You are being present with all of
those vibrations. You are feeling your skin. You are feeling the Earth beneath your feet.
Take a walk and do something for your body and ask it to lead you to a more conscious
embodiment. Every step you take, ask your body how to do this. Be one hundred
percent present with your body. Ask your body . . . "Body, what else can you show me?"
How much more can I receive from you?" "What else do you know that I am refusing
to know?" and "What's beyond this?" The only thing that has been in the way . . . is you.

**Everything that does not allow for you to do this today, will you destroy and
un-create it all?**
Right, Wrong, Good, Bad, POC, POD, All 9, Shorts, Boys and Beyonds™.

When you feel pain in your body, is it really pain, or is it just your body trying to tell
you something? Whenever you feel pain in your body, the first thing to look at is how
expanded are you? Are you being as big as the Universe? If you're not, you can expand
out as big as the Universe and beyond. Sometimes when you experience pain in your
body, your body is saying, "Hey, we need more space!" You can also ask "What generative energy, space and consciousness can I contribute to you to allow this to dissipate?

Your body will start adjusting itself and you will be in communion and there will be no pain. Is pain a creation or is it real? It's a creation. The only thing your body can do when you don't listen to the feather touch of awareness it sends you is turn up the intensity, which equals pain.

Everywhere you have created a relationship with your body that is more like an argument everywhere your body had been turning up the intensity for you to listen to it, will you destroy and un-create it all?
Right, Wrong, Good, Bad, POC, POD, All 9, Shorts, Boys and Beyonds™.

In a session with a very potent being, he he shared with me that he used the tools for creating a communion with his body, he was aware that he had a lot of internal resistance with his body, and the steps I was giving him to change his body. He discovered he downplayed the whole thing and was trying to convince himself that it really wasn't important to listen to his body. Through this he also was able to see all the other places in his being where he was shutting off his awareness. I asked him "How much have you decided that you will never really get anything that you truly desire?" With that decision he has to just accept what he is handed. He came to the awareness that he hadn't been willing to allow himself to fully receive much of anything, especially messages and communion with his body. I explained to him that when resistance comes up, it's there in place to prevent him from having the awesome life he truly desires and when that happens he can always choose something else.

Resistance is the unwillingness to choose. When you resist something, you are just resisting choosing for you. Everywhere resistance comes up which is the resistance that you put up in order not to have your phenomenal life and getting everything you desire out of life, will you destroy and un-create it all now?
Right, Wrong, Good, Bad, POC, POD, All 9, Shorts, Boys and Beyonds™.

If you ever feel like you are having a hard time using any of these tools or applying these secrets of the Universe in your life, you can always ask, "What information am I missing here?" If you still feel stuck with something you're clearing, ask some more questions. It could be that the energy is coming up to be cleared, or the whole thing is a lie, which you think is true. In that case, just acknowledge that it's a lie and it will go away.

Remember, you are not the world around you. If you ever define something as always your problem, like "I never have money" and that is the definition of you, then you will always go out into the Universe and find everybody that has that problem with money and try and work on it. You will always have that awareness and always be trying to work on everybody's problems for all eternity.

Everywhere you've been working on everybody else's stuff and not just acknowledging you and the difference that you be and that you can choose anything, will you destroy and un-create all of that now? Right, Wrong, Good, Bad, POC, POD, All 9, Shorts, Boys and Beyonds™.

Choosing is trump to everything. You can process on things all day, but until you actually choose differently, your life won't show up as the amazing, awesome life you desire. Sometimes action is required as well. For example, if you want to be a famous singer, but you never sing anywhere except in the shower, it is unlikely you will ever get your record deal, or have a huge concert. But, if you are choosing for you, and you desire to sing, and perform at different venues, and promote yourself and are willing to show up for your life, your life will show up for you. You have to be willing to put everything on the line. "Okay, I'm showing up to be a singer regardless if I fall on my face, make a fool out of myself on national television, if I open my mouth and nothing comes out, I'm still choosing it. From there, if any intensity of energy comes up that feels like you're going to use it to stop you, say, "Come on Universe, is that you all got? You really think that is going to stop me? Ha! Watch me!" You can also ask, "what action is required to put this in place?" Whatever you choose, the Universe will conspire to bring it to fruition. If you choose happiness, the Universe will conspire to make you happy.

You can choose with your body, too. What's really cool, is your body will help you choose and lead you in the direction of your awesome life. What if you were here for your body, your body was here for you, you were here for the Universe, and the Universe was here for you? What if you actually created that partnership where you knew each of you had each other's back? That no matter what went on, you'd still choose for you, you would still have you, you would still receive everything you desire regardless of the world around you. Regardless of where everyone was going, you knew that when it gets a little energetically challenged, not only do you have your back because you will choose for you, but your body and the Universe has your back too. Doesn't that just feel like a fresh breeze of total nurturing and support? And you also know you will support and contribute to your body and the Universe, too.

All the walls that you've put up that don't allow you to have that communion with your body, the planet, and the Universe, will you destroy and un-create it all of them? Right, Wrong, Good, Bad, POC, POD, All 9, Shorts, Boys and Beyonds™.

I'll give you a hint, the Universe and your body have been batting for you the whole time. You are the only one who is batting for the other team. What if your body is not wrong? What if any intensity from your body is not wrong? What if your body has been doing the best it can to be your greatest conscious facilitator? When my body gets around someone who can unlock it, like a great chiropractor, it gives me signals of intensity on the area it would like to be worked on. What if your body has been giving you those signals and you thought your body was bad and wrong for it? You thought, "stupid body, why do you hurt?" Your body knows how to not be the effect of things. You won't ask it to show you how to not be the effect of anything. You keep making it your body's fault instead of knowing that your body is a source of magic, potency, change and contribution. What if your body could be your "mama duck"? What if your body could take your hand and show you just how magical having a body and being here could be? What if your body could show you how to receive everything you desire from your life? Would you be willing to ask it to show you?

PROCESSES SOUP: RANDOM RECIPES TO SET YOU FREE

What secret agenda with conscious communion with your body do you have, based solely and only through the VVR's of this reality are you using to maintain and entrain you never being, knowing, perceiving and receiving the gift that you, your body, and the Universe can all be to each other? Everything that does not allow that, will you destroy and un-create it all?
Right, Wrong, Good, Bad, POC, POD, All 9, Shorts, Boys and Beyonds™.

Day 19 *Secret of the Universe Daily Exercise*

Allowing yourself to be totally present in 10 second increments with your body. If you only have 30 minutes to practice this exercise, that's okay. Give yourself that 30 minutes and every 10 seconds, ask these questions.

QUESTIONS FOR TODAY:

"Body, what do you know that I've been denying that I know or pretending not to know here?"
"Body, what else can you show me about how magnificent you are?"
"Body, you are the king or queen today, how can I serve you?"
"Body, what would it take for us to receive us as the oneness and consciousness of all things?"
"Body, what would it take for me to get out of your way?"

"Body, what energy, space and consciousness can you show me in order to have us not
be at the affect of this judgment and conclusion reality?" "Body, I know you are this
magical awareness of the communion with the Universe, please, can you show me how
to have and receive this?" and if you feel like you're not receiving the information,
"Body, I'm sorry, I've cut off so much awareness to you I can't hear you. Can you give
me the information in a way I can receive it?"

NOTES: _____

_____

_____

_____

_____

_____

_____

_____

_____

_____

_____

_____

_____

_____

_____

_____

_____

_____

Stop . . . See you tomorrow!

Day 20

Having the relationship you truly desire

DAILY EXERCISE:
Today we are going to explore choosing in 10 second increments for your body. So you may wish to do this chapter on a day off. "If I had 10 seconds to choose anything for my body what would I choose?"

This is the secret to getting everything you desire out of your relationships, including your relationship with you, or attracting the person with whom you would like to be in relationship with. Are you excited? Are you getting excited?

Have you ever noticed that this is where things get really sticky? Have you also noticed that not a lot of people on this planet are choosing really beautiful generative relationships?

Would you be willing to receive all the information that would allow you to know, and receive, and have what nobody else is willing to have? Everything that doesn't allow that, will you destroy and un-create it all? Right, Wrong, Good, Bad, POC, POD, All 9, Shorts, Boys and Beyonds™.

In order to receive this information, it is necessary that you step out of your reality, out of the "Pinto®" because otherwise you will feel like this information doesn't fit your reality.

Everything that doesn't allow that, will you destroy and un-create it all? Right, Wrong, Good, Bad, POC, POD, All 9, Shorts, Boys and Beyonds™.

Let's start clearing this, everywhere you have duplicated relationships from the world around you, and thought this is the way it has to be, and this is the way it has to be, and this is the way it has to be, because that is the way it's done here, will you destroy and un-create all that? Right, Wrong, Good, Bad, POC, POD, All 9, Shorts, Boys and Beyonds™.

Okay! Let's examine the way most people do relationships and then let's look at a different possibility.

"Pinto®" relationship = You see somebody across a crowded room, and then you meet, and you hit it off! Your bodies are tingling. You are excited and you think, "Oh yeah! This is what it's all about! This is what it's like to be ALIVE!" Everything they say and do is just so perfect, and both of you are in total gratitude for just showing up in each other's lives. You both think, "God, this is what I have been asking for!" Then your lips get close together for your first kiss and energy is surging through your body. You can hardly breath, and your heart is racing, and you just want it to stay like this forever. Suddenly the world becomes brighter and better. Everything is fun and new. You are smiling, happy, and excited to be alive.

Does any of this sound familiar?

Awe, the beginning of the relationship, it's like the perfect summer lullaby, the blissful winter serenade, the autumn of romance, the spring of the first bloom of the heart.

Next question . . . ready to laugh? Which do you like better? The beginning of a relationship . . . or the end?

The beginning! When there's so much energy present, and you are in total gratitude and adoration, how cool is that? Or do you prefer the end, when there's no more energy and you can't figure out how you lost that "loving feeling?"
Let me guess . . . the beginning.

What if you could have the beginning of your relationship go on for all eternity?

SECRET #1: NEVER JUDGE YOUR PARTNER

In the beginning, do the two of you have any judgments, projections, rejections or expectations of each other? Not Yet. Guess what? Each one of those creates a separation between you and them. It's hard to receive when you've constructed walls of judgments that are keeping you separate.

Everything that brings up for you and your relationship with your partner or yourself, will you destroy and un-create all that?
Right, Wrong, Good, Bad, POC, POD, All 9, Shorts, Boys and Beyonds™.

SECRET #2: NEVER GO TO CONCLUSION

In the beginning have you decided that you are going to spend the rest of your lives together? Not yet. Would that be a move towards a question or a conclusion? Conclusion. That's the first step to losing that "loving feeling." We know choice creates presence. So every conclusion you come to takes you out of choosing to be present and receive in the moment.

Everything that brings up and everywhere you have gone into a conclusion about everyone you're in a relationship with, will you destroy and un-create it all? Right, Wrong, Good, Bad, POC, POD, All 9, Shorts, Boys and Beyonds™.

What do you love best about relationships? The energy. This is the key to the relationship of your dreams that is energetically constantly expanding. When you first meet, you don't have any judgment of each other, and you don't have any conclusions either. Every time you go into judgment and conclusion, you are stepping into the "Pinto®" and the destruction of that very energy you both enjoy. Every time you go to judgment or conclusion, it becomes a separation between the two of you. You can no longer receive each other.

Everything that you just accessed in your Universe and all the judgments and conclusions you have about the person you're trying to be closest to, will you destroy and un-create all that now? Right, Wrong, Good, Bad, POC, POD, All 9, Shorts, Boys and Beyonds™.

SECRET #3: NEVER MAKE YOUR PARTNER SIGNIFICANT

When you first meet, are they so significant in your life that if they left, you would die? Would they take everything that is great about your life away?
No. You haven't made them significant yet.
Which one feels lighter?
My significant other? Or my insignificant other?

What if allowing someone you really care about to be your "insignificant other" was actually a gift to both of you and your relationship and is not a wrongness? Everything that brings up, will you destroy and un-create it all now? Right, Wrong, Good, Bad, POC, POD, All 9, Shorts, Boys and Beyonds™.

Secret #4: Choose Your Partner in 10 Second Increments

What if you choose your partner in 10 second increments? We know that choice creates presence. If you begin choosing your partner in 10 second increments the intensity of presence and energy will take your breath away!

Choice creates presence, and when you choose in 10 second increments, how much of you shows up?

The next time you are going to KISS someone . . . say I am choosing to kiss this person, and see how much of you shows up . . . .

Everything this reality teaches you about "how to do relationships" will eliminate those breath-taking kisses, eradicate the expansion between the two you of you, and extinguish the gratitude that expands your life. Now you know. It's the "Pinto's®" version of relationships that doesn't work, not you. If you began having relationships for you, they would work.

How often have you felt like such a failure, that no matter what you do, you just can't seem to get it right with relationships, so you must be wrong, cursed, unlucky in love, not a winner, or just not the relationship type. Everyone else gets to have one, but not you. Everyone always leaves you in the end. You aren't cut out for it. You always make the wrong choice. Every time you find someone you think maybe this one will be different, maybe this one is . . . "the ONE." Then over time it turns out the way all the other ones did. Does that sound familiar?

Everything that brings up and everywhere you thought YOU didn't work in relationships when the way relationships are done here don't work, will you destroy and un-create it all?
Right, Wrong, Good, Bad, POC, POD, All 9, Shorts, Boys and Beyonds™.

How many of you decided that since relationships didn't work for you, your choice was to choose "no relationship?"
Everything that brings up, will you destroy and un-create all that?
Right, Wrong, Good, Bad, POC, POD, All 9, Shorts, Boys and Beyonds™.

One of the biggest keys to the kingdom of relationship is to never judge your partner.

In order to continuously expand that communion with the person you love, you can't have any judgment of them, or you. It may seem impossible, but, the more you embrace total allowance for your partner and no judgment, the easier it gets. When you have a temporary lapse, and judgment comes in, it will feel very heavy because you are not used to choosing it. It really is quite possible to have a beautiful, orgasmic, ever expanding, nurturing, generative, amazing relationship if there is no judgment. What is more valuable to you, judgment or receiving?

Everywhere you can now allow the generative energy of gratitude, expansion, and receiving as having more value to you than judgment, will you destroy and un-create everything that doesn't allow that to exist?
Right, Wrong, Good, Bad, POC, POD, All 9, Shorts, Boys and Beyonds™.

Absolutely no judgment or conclusion of them or you.

You may feel like, how can we have a future together if we don't judge or conclude we will? Yet, do judgments and conclusions eliminate choice and create limitation? Yes. Is that a choice in 10 second increments or is it one choice to end all choices? Every conclusion eliminates the energy. You are then on auto pilot and have eliminated your presence and receiving.

Everything that brings up, will you destroy and un-create it all?
Right, Wrong, Good, Bad, POC, POD, All 9, Shorts, Boys and Beyonds™.

Did you know relationship actually means the distance between two points? If you were being the oneness and consciousness of all things, would there be a relationship? No, there wouldn't be any separation. So here is another tool to allow your relationship to be ever expanding energetically . . . .

Destroy and un-create your relationship every day.
Right, Wrong, Good, Bad, POC, POD, All 9, Shorts, Boys and Beyonds™.

With this you are destroying and un-creating all the judgments and conclusions that you made about them and you yesterday, today and tomorrow. Everything they are to you, everything you are to them, everything they mean to you, everything you mean to them, and all of the energy of the judgments and conclusions you have in place.
Right, Wrong, Good, Bad, POC, POD, All 9, Shorts, Boys and Beyonds™.

If you are always choosing in 10 second increments, you can live a life of sixty years together and still have breath-taking kisses and huge energy with each other! Most people believe that the energy always fizzles, and it only occurs in the beginning, but it's really just a choice. When you allow yourself to have no judgment or conclusion the energy will always be present.

Here are the 5 elements of intimacy that are the keys to the kingdom to have the relationship you truly desire.

1. HONOR
2. TRUST
3. ALLOWANCE
4. GRATITUDE
5. VULNERABILITY

Here's another secret. If you have these with yourself, someone else can show up and have them with you, too. Have you ever had someone show up that loved and adored you totally? Someone who had so much gratitude for you they wanted to be around you all the time? Do anything for you. Worship the ground you walk on? Let me ask you another question . . . Did you receive them, or did you make them go away? Did you judge them as "milquetoast," a "puppy dog," just a little "too into you"? Or, as soon as they were "in to you," you dismissed them with, "I'm just not attracted to them." If you made them go away, that is because they attempted to give you more than you give you. You can't receive something from someone else that you don't give to yourself. You probably thought, "They're wrong, and crazy! If that were true I would have given it to myself by now."

The first step in having this intimacy with another is to have it with yourself. What if you made the commitment to yourself to have these five things in the forefront of your Universe for you? No matter what, you would always give these five elements to yourself?

KEY TO THE KINGDOM: HONOR YOUR PARTNER

To honor means to treat with regard. It means that you would never treat your mate with disrespect. If someone is flirting with you, and your partner is in the room, and you can feel him getting uncomfortable, are you going to add fuel to the fire? Or politely excuse yourself and let your partner know that there is nothing to be concerned about? If you begin honoring your partner, you will be pleased with the level of trust and gratitude that will continue to grow.

KEY TO THE KINGDOM: TRUST YOUR PARTNER

In this reality, trust is done like blind faith. When people say, "I trust you," they are really cutting off their awareness. Have you ever been in a relationship where you "trusted them?" Two years into the relationship they do or be something and you start to find out who they really are and wonder, "Who am I living with? I don't even know you!" When this occurs you decided you "trusted them," and cut off your awareness to everything you decided they would never do to you. Most people in this situation then decide, "I can't trust myself."

Everywhere you decided you can't trust you because you cut off your awareness of someone else, will you destroy and un-create all that?
Right, Wrong, Good, Bad, POC, POD, All 9, Shorts, Boys and Beyonds™.

What we talk about in regards to trust is, trusting that your partner is going to be exactly who they were yesterday. If you have a partner who always leaves the toilet seat up or down, trust that they are going to continue to do that. That way you stay out of the projections, rejections and expectations Universes.

Key to the kingdom: Be in allowance of your partner.

Allowance means that you never resist or react, or align and agree with anything your partner says or does. When you are in allowance, both of you are energetically free from any limitation. What would it take to be in allowance of everything you say or do?

Key to the kingdom: Have Gratitude.

Gratitude is one of the sweetest keys to the relationship of your dreams. We talk about gratitude instead of love because love has so many different definitions for people. Your mom tells you, "I love you" as she judges you. Your dad tells you "I love you," as he walks out on you. So we like to talk about gratitude. Gratitude doesn't require that your partner choose anything. You are grateful for everything they are and everything they are choosing. You are grateful when they are there, and when they are not. What would it take for you to always be grateful for your partner?

Key to the kingdom: Be vulnerable.

Sometimes people confuse vulnerability with weakness, when it is exactly the opposite. When you allow yourself to be vulnerable, you never put barriers to anything. This means you are "tapped into" or receiving nine hundred and ninety nine percent of the Universe. If you put up barriers, you are creating separation and not fully receiving. Every judgment or conclusion is a barrier that doesn't allow you to be vulnerable.

Having instead of wanting . . . .

This is a really bizarre program and it is running around in people's Universe like a mad disease. You know that song by the The Rolling Stones . . . "You Can't Always Get What You Want?" The program in this reality is called, you want what you can't have. Because the only things you desire are the things you have decided you can't have, which keeps everything you desire in the "I can't have it" category because then you wouldn't desire it.

Everywhere you have bought that program, I want what I can't have, for all eternity, about relationships, about money, about clients, about success, about everything . . . Will you destroy and un-create all that?
Right, Wrong, Good, Bad, POC, POD, All 9, Shorts, Boys and Beyonds™.

Wanting, needing, lacking, deserving and making things significant are the ways you push what you would like to show up out of your life. If you had money, would you want it? No, you would have it. Would you need it? No, you would have it. Would you lack it, or make it significant? No, you would have it. So anytime you are doing any of these energies, you are actually pushing whatever it is you desire, out of your life.

What would it be like to invite, embrace, and enjoy the energy of "having?" Having is more like breathing. Do you deserve to breathe, or do you just breathe? You just breathe.

Everywhere you think "wanting" is more valuable to you then "having" will you destroy and un-create all that?
Right, Wrong, Good, Bad, POC, POD, All 9, Shorts, Boys and Beyonds™.

What secret agenda for wanting and desiring what you've decided you can't have, are you using to validate everybody else's realities? Everything that brings up, will you destroy and un-create it all now?
Right, Wrong, Good, Bad, POC, POD, All 9, Shorts, Boys and Beyonds™.

What creation of the longing, needing, and the wanting what you can't have, because it hurts so good, are you using to validate everyone else's realities?
Right, Wrong, Good, Bad, POC, POD, All 9, Shorts, Boys and Beyonds™.

This is so cool. Now we are introducing a new energy with this, and all of a sudden you can realize that you are the one who is actually pushing everything that you truly desire out of your life. As long as you have this program running, you won't choose anything unless it's out of your reach, so that you long for it and want it and desire it always, which has nothing to do with having. How often do you want the guy or girl that is out of your reach? Do you realize you create them out of your reach so that you want them?

If they were right in front of you, you'd be turning and running the other direction. Talk about driving a "Pinto®" in the wrong direction!

Everything that brings up will you destroy and un-create it all now?
Right, Wrong, Good, Bad, POC, POD, All 9, Shorts, Boys and Beyonds™.

That is the joke of the "Pinto®" reality. Every construct, every matrix, every everything is designed to totally have you driving the "Pinto®" in the wrong direction and the only thing you can do from there is judge you because you just don't work. Except, it's not meant to work, it never has been.

Everything that brings up and everything you just acknowledged about how you've been trying to make this reality work in relationships, and it just doesn't work for you, will you destroy and un-create all of that now?
Right, Wrong, Good, Bad, POC, POD, All 9, Shorts, Boys and Beyonds™.

What creation of if I have it, I won't want it, because it's boring, are you using to validate everyone else's realities?
Right, Wrong, Good, Bad, POC, POD, All 9, Shorts, Boys and Beyonds™.

Have you ever done that? Once you had what you desired, you no longer desired it and it wasn't exciting for you anymore because you were having it, which to you didn't mean anything, so you had to find something else to want?
Right, Wrong, Good, Bad, POC, POD, All 9, Shorts, Boys and Beyonds™.

There is a trick about wanting that nobody allows themselves to know or have. If you want something, you won't allow yourself to have it. As you might know I am a singer/songwriter. I used to want a record deal really bad. I used to want it, which means I didn't have it, because wanting means to lack. I was continually wanting a record deal, and I asked for it a billion times. Finally, I realized, hmmm, maybe I could use the Access Consciousness™ tools and processes here. I destroyed and un-created all of the conclusions I had about a record deal and all of the wanting of "it." Literally, once I did that, it showed up in twenty-four hours! Then for the next six weeks I was on cloud nine. It was like everything was heaven. This kind of feels like falling in love, I was getting everything I had wanted in life. The sun was brighter, the air was clearer, everything was great. But, as soon as that energy began to wear off, I realized that I started wanting something else. Then I was telling myself, "sure, I have a record deal, but now I need a great relationship, and then I got it! It's not about the "thing," it's about the energy. If you want something, and then you get it, you are just going to transfer that energy of wanting onto something else, if wanting is more valuable to you than having.

What secret agenda with wanting do you have that maintains and entrains the eternal and perpetual search for what it is you truly desire, while never allowing yourself to have it?

Everything that brings up, will you destroy and un-create it all now?

Right, Wrong, Good, Bad, POC, POD, All 9, Shorts, Boys and Beyonds™.

You feel like you are having a life when you're longing for someone. You feel like you are having a life when you're longing for that thing to show up, and that is valuable to some people. Because we are taught, you can't have everything, you have to want everything.

Everything that brings up, will you destroy and un-create it all?

Right, Wrong, Good, Bad, POC, POD, All 9, Shorts, Boys and Beyonds™.

What secret agenda with your life do you have that maintains and entrains the romance of wanting, needing and longing, as if that is living?

Right, Wrong, Good, Bad, POC, POD, All 9, Shorts, Boys and Beyonds™.

It's like the Prince and the Princess

It's like the Prince and the Princess. The Princess is up in the castle and the Prince can't get to her, and, oh, the romance of longing and wanting. Just look at the Romeo and Juliet story, they just love each other, but . . . it just can't be and they will never get to have each other, and it hurts so good, and if they can't be together than they would rather just die.

Everything that brings up and everywhere you have bought into that version of love, will you destroy and un-create it all?

Right, Wrong, Good, Bad, POC, POD, All 9, Shorts, Boys and Beyonds™.

It's like the cat and mouse game, or a dog chasing its tail. You have the motivation to keep chasing your tail, and you keep chasing it and chasing it, and you'll never get it, but wanting it is more valuable than having it. It's really bizarre. If all you are doing is wanting, whenever you have it, you will throw it away or invalidate it somehow.

Everything that brings up, will you destroy and un-create it all?

Right, Wrong, Good, Bad, POC, POD, All 9, Shorts, Boys and Beyonds™.

The next step...

First acknowledge for you that the energy of "having" is more valuable to you then the energy of "wanting." Okay, now that you are actually going to have your amazing life that you truly desire, it's time to celebrate having!

CELEBRATE HAVING

When things begin to show up in your life, celebrate that they are there! Enjoy it, relish in it! Buy a bottle of champagne with some friends and actually celebrate having your life! What if you begin receiving, having, enjoying and celebrating all that you are willing to let yourself have! By celebrating the "having" you're letting the Universe know what you desire and it will bring you more "having."

Everything that doesn't allow that, will you destroy and un-create it all?
Right, Wrong, Good, Bad, POC, POD, All 9, Shorts, Boys and Beyonds™.

How much of your life do you not allow yourself to celebrate because, you are always waiting for the other shoe to drop or something horrible to happen? How much did your parents teach you to be ready for disappointment? "Not all that glitters is gold," "you can't have your cake and eat it, too," and all of those kind of sayings. How much has that taught you how to not be the energy of having?

Everything that doesn't allow that, will you destroy and un-create it all?
Right, Wrong, Good, Bad, POC, POD, All 9, Shorts, Boys and Beyonds™.

Everywhere you have been eliminating your receiving based on all of those points of view to validate everybody else's realities, will you destroy and un-create all of that now?
Right, Wrong, Good, Bad, POC, POD, All 9, Shorts, Boys and Beyonds™.

Relationship of your dreams...

If you would like someone to show up in your life that would actually blow your Universe open, ask, "What would it take for someone to show up in my life that is nurturing, caring, kind, expansive, joyful, and would expand my life and my money flows?" All you have to do is ask that question, and then begin working on the relationship with you. Because whatever relationship you have with you, is literally what you will allow yourself to receive from the Universe. Honor you, be grateful for you, be in total vulnerability with you, trust you, and don't judge you. The more honor, trust, vulnerability, allowance and gratitude you have with you, the more the Universe can deliver someone who will give it to you as well.

Make a demand

Now that you are out of your wanting and longing phase, you can make a demand on the Universe. You just simply demand to the Universe, I am having this. The Universe, will gift it to you.

P.S. . . . you don't need to ask or demand over and over . . . the energy of having, is the energy of having . . . just have your beautiful life and living.

Make a list of all the "wanting" you have been doing

My wants...

1. I want _____. Now say out loud "I have _____!"
Everything that doesn't allow that, Right, Wrong, Good, Bad, POC, POD, All 9, Shorts, Boys and Beyonds™.

2. I want _____. Now say out loud "I have _____!"
Everything that doesn't allow that, Right, Wrong, Good, Bad, POC, POD, All 9, Shorts, Boys and Beyonds™.

3. I want _____. Now say out loud "I have _____!"
Everything that doesn't allow that, Right, Wrong, Good, Bad, POC, POD, All 9, Shorts, Boys and Beyonds™.

4. I want _____. Now say out loud "I have _____!"
Everything that doesn't allow that, Right, Wrong, Good, Bad, POC, POD, All 9, Shorts, Boys and Beyonds™.

5. I want _____. Now say out loud "I have _____!"
Everything that doesn't allow that, Right, Wrong, Good, Bad, POC, POD, All 9, Shorts, Boys and Beyonds™.

6. I want _____. Now say out loud "I have _____!"
Everything that doesn't allow that, Right, Wrong, Good, Bad, POC, POD, All 9, Shorts, Boys and Beyonds™.

7. I want _____. Now say out loud "I have _____!"

Everything that doesn't allow that, Right, Wrong, Good, Bad, POC, POD, All 9, Shorts, Boys and Beyonds™.

8. I want _____. Now say out loud "I have _____!"

Everything that doesn't allow that, Right, Wrong, Good, Bad, POC, POD, All 9, Shorts, Boys and Beyonds™.

9. I want _____. Now say out loud "I have _____!"

Everything that doesn't allow that, Right, Wrong, Good, Bad, POC, POD, All 9, Shorts, Boys and Beyonds™.

10. I want_____. Now say out loud "I have _____!"

Everything that doesn't allow that, Right, Wrong, Good, Bad, POC, POD, All 9, Shorts, Boys and Beyonds™.

Move into the energy of having . . . Just say to the Universe and yourself . . . I am having!

Do something today to celebrate you having your amazing life, your amazing relationship, more money, more joy, more fun, more of everything, more than you could have asked for or imagined! Choose to have, and celebrate YOU! Celebrate the willingness to have. Celebrate that you have read this book. Celebrate that you have taken these steps. Celebrate that you now have 20 Secrets of the Universe, and that you are choosing to have the life you truly desire!

Congratulations, and remember this is only the beginning of the eternity of expansive, phenomenal consciousness, and dreams all coming true, and the beginning of YOU having more of YOU! I am so grateful for you and all that you are willing to be and have and I am so excited for your new and abundant, rich, rewarding living! Can I get a big WAHOO? How does it get any better than this?

By the way, in case you didn't know it, YOU totally ROCK!

PROCESSES SOUP: RANDOM RECIPES TO SET YOU FREE

What secret agenda with never allowing yourself to have, based solely and only on the virtual vibrational realities of this reality, are you using in order to maintain and entrain the rightness and wrongness of everything you've learned about what you thought you required to live on this planet.

Everything that brings up, will you destroy and un-create it all?
Right, Wrong, Good, Bad, POC, POD, All 9, Shorts, Boys and Beyonds™.

What secret agenda with "stop asking questions, you ask too many questions" are you using to stop you? Everything that brings up, will you destroy and un-create it all?
Right, Wrong, Good, Bad, POC, POD, All 9, Shorts, Boys and Beyonds™.

What secret agenda with the seduction and satisfaction of conclusion, based solely and only on the virtual vibrational realities of this reality, are you using in order to maintain and entrain never allowing yourself to receive the totality of what you could be and receive if you lived in and as the question?
Everything that brings up, will you destroy and un-create it all?
Right, Wrong, Good, Bad, POC, POD, All 9, Shorts, Boys and Beyonds™.

Day 20 ∞ Secret of the Universe Daily Exercise

For today, celebrate and embrace having! When you celebrate having, the Universe gifts you more having!

Everything in this reality is about wanting and longing, as if that is the valuable product. If you celebrate having, you will create more having!

Another exercise for today is pondering this question, "If I was to create a relationship that was just for me, just for fun, what would I create?

NOTES: _____

_____

_____

_____

_____

_____

Stop . . . See you tomorrow!

Day 21

The Love of your life . . . is You!

DAILY EXERCISE:
You are the LOVE of your life. Your life and the Universe is here to LOVE you . . . Ask, "What can I be, do, have, create, generate, choose or change today that would allow me to choose me as being the love of my own life?"

The LOVE of your life . . . is YOU!

This is one of the biggest, best kept secrets of all time. It's the icing on the cake. This is the secret of the Universe that you always keep hidden from you, but if you had it, everything would be easy, everything would be joyful, and everything would work. The Love of your life is you. The secret ingredient is you, and the love of your life and living is you.

How much have you eliminated your adoration, care, and love for you, your body and your life? Everything that doesn't allow that will you destroy and un-create it all? Right, Wrong, Good, Bad, POC, POD, All 9, Shorts, Boys and Beyonds™.

What creation of never being the love of your life are you using to validate everyone else's realities? Everything that brings up will you destroy and un-create it all now? Right, Wrong, Good, Bad, POC, POD, All 9, Shorts, Boys and Beyonds™.

What secret agenda with learning to love you, do you have based solely and only on the virtual vibrational realities of this reality, are you using in order to maintain and entrain everything you cannot be, do, have, create and generate, institute and change that would allow you to love and adore you totally?
Everything that brings up will you destroy and un-create it all now?
Right, Wrong, Good, Bad, POC, POD, All 9, Shorts, Boys and Beyonds™.

You are the creator of your life. Wouldn't you love absolutely every aspect of all of your creations? No matter how funny things look or seem, why wouldn't you adore all of it, even if it looks like the little Charlie Brown Christmas tree? It's so beautiful and such a gift, all of it, every single bit. Think of it this way, everything you have chosen in your life up till now, even all of those things that from your point of view were a mistake or a wrongness, has led you to exactly where you are now. This is the part where your life gets its juice, every sensation of why I love what I do, so much is tingling! All of your choices have brought you to this moment now, the moment where you choose so much more and create such a different possibility for you and the world. Now, all of the thorns, all of those so-called problems, "mistakes," judgments and conclusions are like these little jewels in the necklace of you. Every stone was required to get you to this moment! Now just adore this necklace and truly acknowledge it for everything it has brought you, cause it has brought you home to you. How does it get any better than that? Now you are standing at the threshold looking at you on the other side. Will you jump, because you are the one waiting there for you? Now you know, you are everything you desire in life.

Everything you have done to judge any of the choices you have ever made, (cause each one is the gift that brought you here) will you destroy and un-create all of that now? Right, Wrong, Good, Bad, POC, POD, All 9, Shorts, Boys and Beyonds™.

In class, one of my beautiful, bright infinite beings spoke up and shared with us that she had been looking for the love of her life her whole existence, and never found that person. She really believed she was just unfortunate, and that she never would find that person. Wow, interesting point of view, huh? She had never had the awareness that she was that very person she was looking for, and that everyone who had come into her life was reflecting the love she was willing to be for her. After we ran some clearings with her, and unlocked the energy that she truly is, she was bursting laughing and crying at the same time and the entire energy of her life changed. It almost reminded me of one of those Buddha statues where he is laughing and has this big grin.

How many of you have been looking for the "one," "your soul mate," "your twin flame?" What if that someone is you?
Everything that doesn't allow you to have that will you destroy and un-create all that? Right, Wrong, Good, Bad, POC, POD, All 9, Shorts, Boys and Beyonds™.

Even in the places where your life has been a bit bumpy, could you choose to have total gratitude for all of those choices, and just say "yeah, it's a little bumpy here, but apparently it was everything required to give me me!" And I am going to love it, and adore all of it!

Would you be interested in being gratitude twenty-four/seven, three-hundred and sixty-five days of the year, for every moment, of every day from here on out?

Can you list ten things about you or your life or your choices with complete gratitude for you, your being, this life and where you are now because of you . . . .

Who or what have I chosen in my life that I am grateful for?

1. _____
2. _____
3. _____
4. _____
5. _____
6. _____
7. _____
8. _____
9. _____
10. _____

Take a deep breath and infuse the energy of gratitude through every pore of your body and being. (If you're anything like me, you may end up in tears of gratitude.) By the way, YOU were on my list.

Now, this next exercise might be a little bit tougher.

Who or what have I chosen in my life do I think was "wrong?"

1. _____
2. _____
3. _____
4. _____
5. _____
6. _____
7. _____
8. _____
9. _____
10. _____

Go through each one slowly, take a deep breath and infuse the energy of gratitude through every pore of your body and being. Because this is everything you required to get you to this moment where you could finally have you!

You can see each choice, each creation with gratitude, love and adoration. And, now you can receive what a beautiful you and life you have created.

This is a very interesting place to be standing because hardly anyone allows themselves to have this. A lot of people will review their creations and choices and if they feel like they got something right, they will celebrate that rightness a little, but very rarely, if ever, celebrate ALL of the choices and creations as the beautiful package of you. Just take a deep breath and infuse gratitude into who you've chosen to be.

What if you stepped into it totally? What if you stepped into you absolutely loving and adoring you totally? Everything that doesn't allow that to show up, will you destroy and un-create all that now?
Right, Wrong, Good, Bad, POC, POD, All 9, Shorts, Boys and Beyonds™.

Think of your whole creation of life, all of your choices, the ones you really like, and the ones that in the past you would have judged as "wrong." Now, think of a two year old as they are learning to walk. If they fall down, do you get mad, irritated and blame them for not being able to walk right away? No, of course not, you pick them up, give them some love, let them know it's not that big of a deal, kiss them, and encourage them to take some more steps. When they do, you celebrate it with them as if they just uncovered the cure for all dis-eases, and they are going to receive the Nobel Prize. Imagine if you were this energy with you all the time? You know, you really are adorable, infinitely adorable. What if you allowed yourself to trip and saw it as adorable?

Everywhere you're not allowing yourself to see the things you think are mistakes and wrong are actually adorable, and that you can always choose differently if you choose, will you destroy and un-create it that all now?
Right, Wrong, Good, Bad, POC, POD, All 9, Shorts, Boys and Beyonds™.

You can also ask to have the awareness to not choose something again if it isn't what you truly want. Fantastic, and guess what, if you do, it's still adorable and you are still in love with you.

Everything that doesn't allow that, will you destroy and un-create it all?
Right, Wrong, Good, Bad, POC, POD, All 9, Shorts, Boys and Beyonds™.

What if you thought everything you ever said and did was adorable? What if it took you forty-five minutes in the morning just to leave your bathroom mirror because you were looking at your adorable face? Have you ever fell in love and wanted to stay in bed all day just to stare in their eyes with adoration? Why can't you have that with you? Right now, go to the mirror and play that game with you. Stare in your beautiful eyes and pull in the energy of gratitude, love and adoration. Talk to you as if you were your own nurturing, caring and kind lover.

Here is another secret, what occurs when you love you is that everyone else who meets you, loves you, too. If ever there is someone who dislikes you, you are just one hundred percent okay with that, and if they ever change their mind, then wonderful. If they don't, you don't care because you love and adore you.

Everything that doesn't allow that, will you destroy and un-create it all?
Right, Wrong, Good, Bad, POC, POD, All 9, Shorts, Boys and Beyonds™.

Will you destroy and un-create everything you refuse to be for you, everything you refuse to receive for you, everything you will not allow yourself to know about you and perceive about the totality of who you truly be?
Right, Wrong, Good, Bad, POC, POD, All 9, Shorts, Boys and Beyonds™.

What if you knew who you truly are? What would that be like? What if you actually knew how amazing and wonderful and brilliant you truly are? And what if you actually knew what was true for you?

Everywhere you have eliminated that awareness of you, will you destroy and un-create all of that?
Right, Wrong, Good, Bad, POC, POD, All 9, Shorts, Boys and Beyonds™.

What are some of the things you are unwilling to receive about who you truly are?
List 6 of your wonderful attributes.

1. _____
2. _____
3. _____
4. _____
5. _____
6. _____

Can you now see that you are the biggest gift ever that you could receive?

In essence, you have assumed, or adopted the idea that you were wrong, when in truth, you are and always have been a gift of magnitude! Now you can have all of that, all of the time! Here is another secret, there is even more! Everywhere you can receive how amazing you are, you can receive it everywhere and from everyone!

Here is a fun exercise, everywhere you have been picking up on the mass collective consciousness and defining yourself from that, will you destroy and un-create it all now?
Right, Wrong, Good, Bad, POC, POD, All 9, Shorts, Boys and Beyonds™.

Just for fun, you can get a can or bowl, and write down all of the ridiculous ideas, definitions and judgments you had previously assumed were you. Then start a fire in the bowl and throw all the papers in. Laugh with wild abandon, as you watch the flames burn, and acknowledge just how much fun all of your life and living has been, even the trauma and drama. Toast to the comedic sit-com expression of a previously polarized version of you. Now embrace the entirety of the new you. You can even create an alias if you wish, because now you are a new being, the being you be.

The artist formally known as _____.

As you open your new eyes to you and the world around you, you will see you are the gift for you. You are that infinite being as big as the Universe. You are that beautiful being that is sweet, soft, amazing and vulnerable. What if you could blow your own mind of how much you love and adore you every day, if you were just willing to choose it, would you choose to?

When you know just how infinitely grateful, caring and nurturing you really be, you can choose it at anytime.

YOU are the LOVE of your LIFE . . . .

And when you choose to love and adore you, the Universe will conspire to bring people to you who love and adore you too. If some don't, it doesn't matter to you, because you have you. This is the key to the kingdom and I am so grateful and utterly amazed by your willingness to choose a life full of love and adoration of and for you, full of your dreams coming true, full of your brilliant radiance, full of your beautiful potency.
YOU are the LOVE of your LIFE . . . .

YOU are the LOVE of your LIFE ....
YOU are the LOVE of your LIFE ....

By choosing so much more than you ever thought was possible, you are creating even more LOVE for you, more potency for you and more expansion for you and the world. You are the Superhero. You are the infinite gift that just keeps gifting. You are the infinite being and infinite receiver.

You are here to change the world, by changing your world, and here is another secret, you already have. Is time real or is time a construct? A construct, right? So every time you run one of these clearing statements and choose to change you, you are undoing it for everyone you bought and sold it to through all time, space, dimensions and realities. You undo these limitations for at least 350,000 other people. You are a leader, a visionary, the one in the mirror who can make a difference anywhere.

This has been an extraordinary journey, that will continue to gift to you. You can use this book and these secrets over and over and will eternally expand and unlock you more. I recommend that you start at Day 1 again. This time through, at the end of the Day 1 audio, put in the Advanced Lesson to add to your journey. The Advanced Lessons are additional audios to be added once you have been through the program once. I facilitated Advanced Lessons for Days 1-9. From Day 10 on the Advanced information is incorporated into the regular day's program. Each time you do a daily secret and exercise you'll find even more secrets hidden just for you.

Welcome to your new self, the self you always knew was possible, and dreamed about becoming. How did I get so lucky to be on this planet with you?

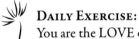 **DAILY EXERCISE:**
You are the LOVE of your life. Your life and the Universe is here to LOVE you ... What can you be, do, have, create, generate, choose or change today that you would allow you to choose you for the love of your life?

Whatever that might be, begin now, right now, in this very moment.
Be the LOVE of your life, and allow your life and the Universe to LOVE YOU ....

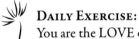 **DAILY QUESTION:** If am the LOVE of my life and my life and the Universe is the love of me, what energy would I choose and be for me right now?
(Ask, and choose this in 10 second increments.)

PROCESSES SOUP: RANDOM RECIPES TO SET YOU FREE

What secret agenda with learning to love you do you have, based solely and only on the virtual vibrational realities of this reality, are you using in order to maintain and entrain everything you cannot be, do, have, create, generate, institute and change, that would allow you to be the love of your life?

Everything that doesn't allow that, will you destroy and un-create it all?

Right, Wrong, Good, Bad, POC, POD, All 9, Shorts, Boys and Beyonds™.

What secret agenda with remembering your past, based solely and only on the virtual vibrational realities of this reality do you have that maintains and entrains the constant state of judgment in order to have you or the life you want, (from your point of view) which is actually the elimination of you?

Everything that brings up, will you destroy and un-create it all?

Right, Wrong, Good, Bad, POC, POD, All 9, Shorts, Boys and Beyonds™.

What are you unwilling to perceive, know, be and receive about the real you, based solely and only on the virtual vibrational realities of this reality, are you using to maintain and entrain never allowing yourself to be, know, perceive and receive the true you, you actually came to this planet to be?

Everything that brings up, will you destroy and un-create it all?

Right, Wrong, Good, Bad, POC, POD, All 9, Shorts, Boys and Beyonds™.

NOTES: _____

_____

_____

_____

_____

_____

_____

_____

My beautiful friends,

What a grand and glorious journey this has been! We have shared so much in the last 21 days together. We have laughed . . . we have cried . . . we have unlocked those places where we've judged or limited ourselves, so that we could begin to have the gift and contribution we truly came to this planet to be.

It is my greatest hope, that after this 21 day program you will begin to have an awareness of the real you. Not the "you" you judge . . . the real you. This beautiful, talented, amazing, gentle, sweet, caring, and brilliant infinite being you truly be. You are far greater than anything you can imagine. What if what you are truly looking for . . . is you? May this be the beginning of the journey of finding out just how truly phenomenal you really are.

As I sit here and write these last words of this book, tears of gratitude are streaming down my face.
Thank you for your courage . . . Thank you for your willingness to trust you . . .
Thank you for choosing consciousness in a world where most people don't even know it exists. You choice to choose something greater then what the rest of the world is willing to receive is a gift and contribution so great the impact is beyond comprehensible. No one could run a 4-minute mile until one person could. With every choice for something greater you are being that world-changing leader that will allow the collective consciousness to slip into it with ease.

If you enjoyed this program, I highly, highly, highly . . . did I say highly? recommend all of the Access Consciousness™ Classes. The first time I met the founder of Access Consciousness™ Gary Douglas and Dain Heer I was so grateful I cried all night. It was the first time anyone had ever seen me and truly cared about the real me. I was in such celebration that they actually existed on this planet and I knew in that moment I was going to have all of me.

My target is to gift these Access Consciousness™ tools and processes to as many people as possible as quickly as possible so that we can have a different world. If the world was functioning from consciousness could any of the wars, violence, or devastation occur? If you feel moved to spread these seeds of consciousness, host me in your city, or be a part of our team I invite you to www.rikkazimmerman.com click on "Join The Team."

Thank you for you and the gift you be for the world. I am truly grateful to know you. I wonder what we can change and create in this world together?

Gratefully,

Rikka

❧ Quick Start Guide to Consciousness ❧

WHEN TO USE THIS TOOL	TOOL OR QUESTION TO USE	MORE INFORMATION
Ask this for 3 days for everything. Then if any energy feels heavy. This will allow you to be a walking, talking meditation.	Ask . . . "Who does this belong to?" for 3 days straight. Then ask it for any other energy that isn't working for you.	What if you are 1,000% more aware of the world around you then you think you are? You think everything you think and feel belongs to you. It might be beneficial to you to ask "Who does this belong to?" as a first position to shift any energy.
If "Who does this belong to?" doesn't change the energy totally	Run . . . "Everywhere I bought this as mine, and everything I've bought based on it ever since, I will now destroy and un-create it all. RWGBPPA9SBB"	You may have already decided it was yours.
To change any heavy energy or if you don't know what tool to use	Say . . . "All of life comes to me with ease, joy and glory!" over and over again until the energy changes.	Say it 10x in the morning and 10x at night. If you ever don't know what tool to use, this is a great one. Glory means: exuberant expression and abundance of life.
If you would like any situation to get even better	Ask . . . "How does it get any better than this?" Guess what? It will.	You can ask this for anything and everything: if you get a promotion, if you get a flat tire, if you get a new client, if you get bad news. You're telling the universe, "I'm grateful for everything I've been gifted and I'm willing to receive more, thank you."

❧ Quick Start Guide to Consciousness ❧

WHEN TO USE THIS TOOL	TOOL OR QUESTION TO USE	MORE INFORMATION
When it feels like you have no other choice, or limited choices	Ask . . . "What else is possible?"	The question creates possibilities. The answer eliminates possibilities. When you ask, "What else is possible?" What else is possible begins showing up.
If you feel contracted in any way, or are experiencing "pain" in your body	Expand Out. Close your eyes. Now expand out as big as the room that you're in. Now expand out as big as the city, the state, the country, the world, universes and beyond. Does your body feel more nurtured?	When you are expanded you can't be impacted by anyone else's thoughts, feelings or emotions. Your body likes it when you are expanded, too!
If you are in resistance, getting upset or angry in any way	Practice being in allowance. Run, "Everything that I am resisting or re-acting to or aligning and agreeing with here, I'll now destroy and un-create all that. RWGBPPA9SBB"	If you never resist or react or align and agree with any energy you will be free to choose. Ever resisted someone who cut you off in traffic? Do you notice when you resist how much longer it takes to dissipate the energy?
If someone makes you angry immediately when you meet them	Run . . . "All my oaths, vows, commealties, fealties, and commitments from any lifetime, I will destroy and un-create them all RWGBPPA9SBB"	There may be oaths, vows or commitments from other lifetimes coming up.
If anything makes you feel heavy, it's a lie	The truth will always make you feel lighter and a lie will always make you feel heavier.	Once you acknowledge the lie, everything will get lighter. Trying to make lies true will "hurt."

❧ Quick Start Guide to Consciousness ❧

WHEN TO USE THIS TOOL	TOOL OR QUESTION TO USE	MORE INFORMATION
If anger comes up when someone else is talking	Ask . . . "What's the truth and what's the lie spoken, or unspoken?" Once you spot the lie that you're tying to make true, everything will get lighter.	There is a good chance that they are lying to you and you are trying to believe them. Now, they may be lying to themselves, too, so don't take it personally.
If anger comes up when you are thinking or talking	Ask . . . " Is this actually true, or is this a convenient truth I am using to limit me? All the lies I'm trying to make true here, I will destroy and un-create all of them. RWGBPPA9SBB"	There is a good chance that you are lying to you. We call these convenient truths. These are limited beliefs that are "lies" that you are trying to make true.
If you get angry with you	Run . . . "Everywhere I denied my knowing here, I destroy and un-create all that. RWGBPPA9SBB." Then promise to you that you are never going to "deny your knowing" ever again. And next time, listen to the feather touch of your knowing.	When you do something that you know you shouldn't have done, it will make you angry with you.
If you feel angry	Is someone lying to me, am I lying to myself, or am I stepping into a potency? You may just be stepping into a potency. Let's say, you let everyone else take the stage, and you don't. When you demand you are never going to do that again, it can feel like you're angry.	Just allow the anger to flow. Let your friends and family know that it has nothing to do with them. Sometimes moving your body can assist to harness the energy for you instead of suppressing it.

৯৯ Quick Start Guide to Consciousness ৯৯

WHEN TO USE THIS TOOL	TOOL OR QUESTION TO USE	MORE INFORMATION
If someone makes you angry when you meet them	Run . . ."All my oaths, vows, commealties, fealties, and commitments from any lifetime, truth, I destroy and un-create then all RWGBPPA9SBB"	There may be oaths, vows or commitments from other lifetimes coming up.
If someone is being an energy and it makes you angry	Run . . . "Everything that they are willing to be and receive that I am not willing to be and receive, I destroy and un-create all that. RWGBPPA9SBB"	They may be willing to be an energy that you're not willing to be. If someone is being really sexual, and you get angry, that may mean you aren't allowing yourself to be your totality of sexualness.
If you wake up and feel any heaviness at all	First ask, "Who does this belong to? Then ask . . . "Who am I today and what grand and glorious adventures am I having?" "I choose joy!"	You're probably perceiving the radio station of (this reality) everyone else's thoughts, feelings and emotions.
If you wake up and feel tired	Ask . . ."Body, are you tired or am I the one that is tired?"	Sometimes when you sleep, you in essence "go to work." If you ask this, it will assist you in not locking that energy into your body.
If you wake up and feel tired after sleeping next to someone	Run . . ."Body, everything you took out of their universe can we destroy and un-create all that? BHCEEMCS Everything is the opposite of what it appears to be. BHCEEMCS nothing is the opposite of what it appears to be."	You may have done a tremendous amount of healing on their body.

❧ Quick Start Guide to Consciousness ❧

WHEN TO USE THIS TOOL	TOOL OR QUESTION TO USE	MORE INFORMATION
If you feel like you've been hit by a truck after any interaction	Ask . . . "If I was a Superhero, what did I just do here? Everything I'm unwilling to perceive, know, be and receive about this I'll now destroy and un-create it all."	You have far more talents, abilities and capacities then you've ever given yourself credit for. When you don't acknowledge you, it will feel like you've been hit by a truck.
If you're judging yourself	Ask . . . " Who does this belong to? and return everything to sender 10,000x with consciousness" RWGBPPA9SBB	If 98% of your thoughts, feelings and emotions don't belong to you, do you suppose 98% of your judgments don't belong to you, too? When you return something to sender 10,000x with consciousness, you are returning the energy that will unlock the limitation for them, too.
If you're judging yourself	Run . . ."You know what? I'm not going to judge myself here." (about everything) And "You know what? I don't have to be perfect."	Are you trying to be perfect? How many judgments do you have, to decide what's perfect? What if you didn't have to be perfect?
If you're judging your body	Picture a stop sign and just stop. Then choose a generative energy like, "I love my beautiful eyes."	Quitting judging is like quitting smoking. You are addicted to judging you. What if there was nothing judge able about you? What if you gave up judging you today, everyday?

Quick Start Guide to Consciousness

WHEN TO USE THIS TOOL	TOOL OR QUESTION TO USE	MORE INFORMATION
To unravel judgments locked in your body	Run . . ."Everything I have resisted or reacted to or aligned and agreed with that allows any and all of this to exist, I'll now destroy and un-create all that." RWGBPPA9SBB	Judgments lock what you're judging in place. Having no judgment and asking questions with no investment in the outcome creates the change.
If you're judging someone else	Run . . . "POC and POD where I've been there or done that." RWGBPPA9SBB	There hasn't been anything you haven't been or done from any lifetime. The judgment may be coming up because you have the same judgment of you from some lifetime.
If you're judging someone else	Ask . . ."Is this my judgment of them, or their judgment of themselves?"	People wear judgments like neon signs. You may be reading their judgment of themselves.
If you can't sleep	Say . . ."All of life comes to me with ease, joy and glory!" And "Everything is the opposite of what it appears to be. Nothing is the opposite of what it appears to be."	This will allow you to turn your mind off with ease. Also you may want to run the "expand out" exercise.
If you feel like energy is stuck in your body	Run . . ."BCHEMMCS everything is the opposite of what it appears to be. BCHEMMCS nothing is the opposite of what it appears to be."	This is great to run anytime you feel "slimed" with energy.

❧ Quick Start Guide to Consciousness ❧

WHEN TO USE THIS TOOL	TOOL OR QUESTION TO USE	MORE INFORMATION
If you feel like you're being subjected to psychic attack	Run . . ."Everything is the opposite of what it appears to be. Nothing is the opposite of what it appears to be."	People find you based on your judgments of you. This will allow you to shake up your vibration so that people can't locate you. This also works if you're picking up on someone thinking about you.
If you keep playing a conversation over and over again in your head	Ask . . ."Are they thinking about me, or is something about what this person said not true?" If the second one is lighter, run "What is the truth here and what is the aa here spoken, or unspoken." Once you spot the lie everything will get lighter.	They may be thinking about you. If so, run the process above. If you are trying to make something someone said true, that is actually a lie, it will play over and over again in your head until you acknowledge the lie.
If a song is stuck in your head	Run . . . All the secret, hidden, covert, unseen, unsaid, undisclosed and unacknowledged implants and explants, I'll now destroy and un-create all that" RWGBPPA9SBB.	Or for short all the S.H.C.U.U.U.U. implants and explants.
To change anything	Ask these four questions . . . "What is this? What do I do with this? Can I change it? What would it take to change it?"	The question creates possibilities. The answer eliminates possibilities. Asking these four questions can begin changing anything.

∾ Quick Start Guide to Consciousness ∾

WHEN TO USE THIS TOOL	TOOL OR QUESTION TO USE	MORE INFORMATION
If you are immediately "attracted" to someone	Run . . ."All my oaths, vows, commealties, fealties, and commitments from any lifetime, truth, I destroy and un-create them all. RWGBPPA9SBB"	If you run this, then you will not feel compelled to choose anything. It will be a choice from the moment which will allow you to receive more.
To increase intimacy any relationship, fill in the blanks . . . (this can be run for objects or concepts, too, like money)	Ask . . ."What does _____ mean to me? What do I mean to _____? What does sex with _____ mean to me? What does sex with me mean to _____?	If you let go of all the meaning of the person you are in relationship with, would you be closer or further away? Closer, huh? This process will allow you to let go of all the judgments and conclusions that are actually creating separation.
To increase the energy and receiving in any relationship	Run . . ."I destroy and un-create my relationship with _____."	This is a great way to continue creating a new relationship every day.
How to never lose that "loving feeling"	Never judge your partner or create any conclusions about the relationship. Also you can run "I'm choosing to kiss (or be with) this person" and see how much of you shows up?	Choice creates presence. When you choose to be with your partner the energy is extraordinary.
To create more presence	Ask . . ."If I had 10 seconds to receive the rest of my life, what would I choose here? Okay. That 10 seconds is up. If I had 10 seconds to receive the rest of my life, what would I choose here?"	This will allow you to be totally present to receive your life.

❧ Quick Start Guide to Consciousness ❧

WHEN TO USE THIS TOOL	TOOL OR QUESTION TO USE	MORE INFORMATION
If you feel tired or anxious	Ask . . ."Is this mine, someone elses, or something else's?" If you get "something else" contribute energy to the earth three times.	In the mitochondria of your cells you have enough energy to power the city of New York for three months. So, an infinite being could be tired based on what? The earth is requiring our contribution.
If you're having a "bad experience"	Ask . . ."What judgments do I have here? Everything that brings up, I'll now destroy and un-create it all. RWGBPPA9SBB."	You experience your life through your judgments. If you let go of the judgments you'll have a different experience.
If you're having a "bad experience" . . . . To change any dis-ease, illness, or disorder	First . . . destroy and un-create all your points of view about the dis-ease, illness or dis-order. RWGBPPA9SBB. Live in the question about what it would take to change it. Listen to what your body asks you to do or be to change it.	What if your body is more conscious then you? Ask your body, "Body, did you create the dis-ease, illness or disorder? Or did I create the dis-ease illness or dis-order?" Which ever makes you feel lighter is true.
If you feel like you "don't know"	Run . . . "Everything I am un-willing to be, know, perceive and receive about this, I will now destroy and un-create all that. RWGBPPA9SBB"	An infinite being be's, knows, perceives and receives. If you feel like you "don't know," run what you're un-willing to perceive, know, be and receive and it will clear everything you're unwilling to know and your awareness will become clearer.

✎ Quick Start Guide to Consciousness ✎

WHEN TO USE THIS TOOL	TOOL OR QUESTION TO USE	MORE INFORMATION
"Lose weight," or change your body image	First . . . destroy and un-create all your judgments about your body shape. RWGBP PA9SBB. Once you have no point of view, ask your body questions about what it would take to change it. Then, listen to what your body asks you to do or be, in order to change it. For a while, you may need to muscle test everything you eat until you have a clear communication. If any bite doesn't taste like an or-gasm, your body is probably done eating.	What if, what you see in the mirror, is a culmination of your judgments? What if your body is fulfilling your every desire with every judgment you take? What would it take for you to be nurturing, caring, kind, expansive, joyful and the space of no judgment for your body?
If it seems like people are always treating you bad or taking advantage of you	Run, "What energies am I refusing to be, know, perceive and receive that I truly could be, know, perceive and receive that if I would perceive, know, be and receive them, would change all realities and non-realities and manifest as never being able to be dominated, manipulated, controlled or orchestrated by anyone, anything or any energy ever? Everything that doesn't allow that, I will now destroy and un-create all that. RWGBPPA9SBB."	Any energy you are un-willing to be, people will dominate, manipulate and control you with. Would an infinite being be certain energies, or would an infinite being be any energy at will and choice?

❧ Quick Start Guide to Consciousness ❧

WHEN TO USE THIS TOOL	TOOL OR QUESTION TO USE	MORE INFORMATION
If you have asked for something and it hasn't shown up, have you made it significant?	Ask . . . "Am I making this significant? Everything I have made significant here I will now destroy and un-create all that. RWGBPPA9SBB"	Ever notice how when you place no significance on what you've asked for it shows up instantaneously? And when you make it significant it takes forever or never shows up? When you make something significant are you being the energy of "having it" or "not having it?"
If you would like for something to show up in your life	Ask . . . "What would it take for _____ to show up? What generative energy, space and consciousness can I be for _____ to show up?"	Ask and you shall receive is actually true. What if all you had to do was ask? The second question will allow you to step into the energy of "having" whatever it is you're asking for.
If you have asked for something and it hasn't shown up? What if you didn't have to figure it out?	Run . . . "Everything I have figured out here, I will now destroy and un-create all that. RWGBPPA9SBB."	How often has figuring it out actually worked? What if the "how" was not your job. What if everything you figure out is the limitation that keeps the universe from being able to gift to you?
If you feel like you are choosing something that might not work for you	Ask . . . "Would an infinite being truly choose this?"	If an infinite being wouldn't choose this, then why would you?

⤐ Quick Start Guide to Consciousness ⤏

WHEN TO USE THIS TOOL	TOOL OR QUESTION TO USE	MORE INFORMATION
If you are doing blame, shame, regret, jealously, fear or guilt	Run . . . "All the distractor implants that are creating blame, shame, regret, jealously, and guilt as real and true in my reality, I will now destroy and un-create all that. RWGBPPA9SBB."	The truth will always make you feel lighter. A lie will always make you feel heavier. Do any of those make you feel lighter? What if they are all programs to distract you from being present?
If "fear" is coming up	Ask . . . "Is this fear or is this excitement?" Then say, "Universe, you really think this is going to stop me? Watch this." And choose.	Neurologically there is no difference between "fear" and "excitement." What if when fear shows up, that is actually you showing up as the potency of you?

These tools and questions have come from Access Consciousness™, (founder Gary M. Douglas)

NOTES: _____

_____

_____

_____

_____

Glossary

BE

In this book, we sometimes use the word be in an unconventional way, as in the question, "What generative energy, space and consciousness can I be that would allow me to be the energy of having and accumulating money I truly be?

We use the word be here because if you can't be money, you can't have money.

Why don't we say, "the money I truly am?" Because am is an evidentiary contrivance of beingness. Am is a contrived point of view. Be refers to infinite being, where you can be all aspects of everything you could potentially be.

CLEARING STATEMENT (POC/POD)

The clearing statement we use in Access Consciousness™ is:

Right, Wrong, Good, Bad, POC, POD, All 9, Shorts, Boys and Beyonds™.
Stands for a series of questions designed to unlock the energy of whatever is limiting you. It's easy, fun, dynamic and you can fill in the blanks and apply it in changing any area of your life.

RIGHT AND GOOD
Stands for: How have we made _____ right, good, perfect, and correct?

WRONG AND BAD
Stands for: How have we made _____ wrong, terrible, awful, mean, and vicious?

POC
Stands for Point of Creation: What we're looking to do is clear where we planted the seed of limitation of _____ in any lifetime. If we destroy the seed does it then destroy the roots, tree, fruit and everything you've built based on it ever since then?

POD
Stands for Point of Destruction: In order to hold any limitation in existence we have to be destroying us in order to hold it in place. How much have we been destroying us in order to keep the limitation of _____ in place?

ALL NINE

Stands for: How does _____ diminish us? How does _____ make us absolutely, totally, irrevocably, infinitely, utterly and eternally meaningless? What are the rewards that make _____ right, good, perfect, and correct or wrong, terrible, awful, mean, and vicious? In _____ what choices have we made or are we making? In _____ what creations created the commitments to the creation of our limitations? In _____ how many controls, definitions, limitations, forms, structures, significances, linearities, & concentricities of us hold this in existence? In _____ what are we unwilling to destroy that holds this in existence?

SHORTS

Stands for: What does _____ mean to us? How do we make _____ meaningless? What are we punishing ourselves with in regards to _____? What are the rewards of _____?

BOYS

Stands for: All the areas of our lives we've tried to handle something continuously with no effect. We would like to unlock the energy of the limitation even if you don't even know cognitively where it comes from.

BEYONDS

Stands for: All the feelings & sensations that take us out of being present and aware. Have you ever gotten a cell phone bill that was $900 instead of your $34 plan? That's a beyond. When any energy comes up you can say, "Everything that brings up will you destroy an un-create all that?

RIGHT, WRONG, GOOD, BAD, POD, POC, ALL 9, SHORTS, BOYS & BEYONDS™

We say "destroy and un-create" because we are destroying our limitations, and un-creating everywhere you have created the limitation.

CONFLICTUAL UNIVERSE (also called a conflictual reality or a conflictual paradigm)

It's a point of view that contains conflicting elements. It's a problem. For example, were you told as a child that the love of money is the root of evil? And are you refusing to be evil? That's a conflictual Universe.

EVIDENTIARY CONTRIVANCE

It is a contrived point of view, a viewpoint you have developed. It is when you say, "This is the way money ought to be," or "This is the way things ought to work with money." You consider that you would like something to be a certain way and then you gather evidence to try and make it right. It is not looking at what is.

A Note to Readers

Access Consciousness™ is an energy transformation program which links seasoned wisdom, ancient knowledge and channeled energies with highly contemporary motivational tools. Its purpose is to set you free by giving you access to your truest, highest self.

The information, tools and techniques presented in this book are just a small taste of what Access Consciousness™ has to offer. There is a whole Universe of processes and classes.

If there are places where you can't get things in your life to work the way you know they ought to, then you might be interested in attending an Access Consciousness™ class, workshop or locating a facilitator. They can work with you to give you greater clarity about issues you haven't yet overcome. Access Consciousness™ processes are done with a trained facilitator, and are based on the energy of you and the person with whom you're working with.

WWW.RIKKAZIMMERMAN.COM

Other Access Consciousness™ Books

Conscious Parents Conscious Kids
This book is a collection of narratives from children immersed in living with conscious awareness.

Money is Not the Problem, You Are
Offering out-of-the-box concepts with money. Its not about money. It never is. Its about what you're willing to receive.

Talk To The Animals
Did you know that every animal, every plant, every structure on this planet has consciousness and desires to gift to you?

Embodiment: The Manual You Should Have Been Given When You Were Born
Introducing you to the awareness that there really is a different choice.

Sex Is Not a Four Letter Word but Relationship Often Times Is
Funny, frank, and delightfully irreverent, this book offers readers an entirely fresh view of how to create great intimacy and exceptional sex.

Magic. You are it. Be it
Magic is about the fun of having the things you desire. The real magic is the ability to have the joy that life can be.

www.AccessConsciousness.com

Access Consciousness™ Seminars, Workshops & Classes

If you liked what you read in this book and are interested in attending Access Consciousness™ seminars, workshops or classes, then for a very different point of view, read on and sample a taste of what is available.

Access Consciousness™ Bars Class

ONE-DAY

Bars is one of the foundational tools of Access Consciousness™. You will learn a hands-on energetic process, which you will gift and receive during the class. The bars process has created massive amounts of ease and change for people all over the world. The bars consist of 32 points on the head which hold the electrical energetic charge of the thoughts, ideas, beliefs, decisions, and emotions that you have stored in any lifetime about:

Healing, Body, Time, Hopes, Control, Awareness, Creativity, Power, Aging, Sex, Money, and so forth. The bars are activated by a light touch, allowing energy to flow. This creates greater ease in your body and opens new possibilities, freeing the "stuck" areas of your life and allowing you to choose in the present rather than from the past. Every time you gift a bars session to someone, you receive the benefits as well. This class is wonderful for any bodywork practitioners, as well as for people who have always wanted to learn a dynamic energetic process. It is also a way for you to experience receiving, rather than the doing, doing, doing that people are always taught.

PREREQUISITES: None

Access Consciousness™ Foundation Class

TWO-DAY

This class invites you to look at where you reside in the "I have no choice" Universe—to change it! You will gain clarity on how you have used reason, justification, beliefs, and judgments to create your reality, as well as awareness of the energetic structures that are obstructing your ability to change. The clearings you receive from this class will allow you to claim, own, and acknowledge your potency to transform anything that isn't working for you. You will receive tools to recognize truth and lies, to utilize language and energy to generate your life, as well as learning a dynamic hands-on process to heal cellular memory in bodies.

PREREQUISITES: Bars Class

Access Consciousness™ Level One Class

TWO-DAY

This class expands on the possibilities opened in the Foundation class and covers areas of sexualness, money, abundance, and the five elements of intimacy. The clearings allow you to eliminate limitations and distractors, as well as to gain clarity about some of the greatest lies of this reality. You can generate relationships in which you are honored. You may receive greater awareness of infinite beingness and infinite choice, so you can perceive, know, be, and receive with ease. You will also learn another amazing, hands-on body process called MTVSS (molecular terminal valence sloughing system).

PREREQUISITES: BARS & FOUNDATION CLASS

Access Consciousness™ Level 2 and 3 Class

FOUR-DAY

Facilitated by Gary Douglas, the founder of Access, and Dr. Dain Heer

These classes invite you to go beyond this reality and generate your life as phenomenal. The lies of this reality pertaining to the love/hate program, you as a victim, the perfection of success, so-called "disabilities," insane relationships, and eternal sadness will be cleared from your Universe. You will recognize where you have denied joy and happiness from your life and begin to acknowledge yourself as the valuable product. Your talents and abilities will continue to be uncovered, as well as your communion with your body. Choose to step into the potency of allowance and oneness to create change on the planet. Claim the magic that you can create in your life and for others.

PREREQUISITES: BARS CLASS, FOUNDATION & ONE

Access Consciousness™ Body Class

VARIES

In this dynamic hands-on class you will receive and gift hands-on body processes which will shift your body from degenerating itself into generating itself. The processes you learn will create your body and those of your friends and family, to function with more ease and joy. Those attending this class report fewer sicknesses, less pain, and an easier ability to create the body they desire. What would it take for you and your body to be in communion? What else is possible?

Information

For more information on Gary Douglas, Dr. Dain Heer, books and other products; Access Energy Transformation seminars, workshops or classes; class registrations or if you have any questions please visit: www.AccessConsciousness.com

Other Access Consciousness™ Websites

www.DrDainHeer.com (Dain Heer)

www.GaryMDouglas.com

www.Facebook.com/accessconsciousness

www.Twitter.com/accessconscious

Journal

CPSIA information can be obtained at www.ICGtesting.com
261288BV00004B/1/P